DATE DUE			
Feb 23 '72			
May 23 '72			
Nov 8 '72			
Nov 29 '72			

Armed Love

Armed

Love

Elia Katz

Holt, Rinehart and Winston

New York/Chicago/San Francisco

ISBN: 0–03–086709–6
Library of Congress Catalog Card Number: 72–155520
First Edition

Printed in the United States of America

"Together, we are a power as great as our deformities. . . ."

—*The Brain That Wouldn't Die* (1960)

Armed Love

New York

Rateyes and I met her on 86th Street, at two or three
in the morning. We did not know at first she was a
whore. She appeared to be around fourteen years old.
In a cold wind, in a cold pocket on the downslope of
86th Street, she was looking into the window of an
appliance and novelty store. In this window were tiers
of grass that were wet with dew and shone in the sun
bulb that was also there. There were toasters and electric toothbrushes and vibromassage dildos landscaped
on these tiers of grass. Julia was small and gorgeous;
the sun in the window shone on her face, which was
pale Puerto Rican, sharp and slouchless. Every price
was slashed in this window and everything was special
that Julia was studying there. Rateyes and I had as
little to say to one another as any two boys who feel
like getting laid and aren't about to get laid and who
are keeping each other company. There are times when
two friends will walk around in New York saying to
each other, wouldn't it be amazing if two amazing
chicks showed up and they really felt like getting laid?
Then there are times past these times when two friends
will be walking together each feeling he would be doing
a lot better on his own. We were in one of these times,
Rateyes and I. 86th Street has a lot of whores on it.
At the time of morning when this was there are no
girls on that street except whores. Nevertheless, even
with desire and the right to expectation right there at
the fronts of our brains, we did not suspect she was a
whore. We thought she was a fourteen-year-old girl who
needed a toothbrush. We passed her by after only the
shortest time of animating our faces at her. When we

were past her we turned around, not as a team, but each in his own private pride, and she was looking at us. She was smiling and we felt, each in his own private pride, that she was in love with us. Back we rolled, a little up the hill, and surrounded her as only two friends who are trying to beat each other out of a girl can do. "What are you doing looking in this window," said Rateyes, in a mockingly stern tone that referred to her apparent age, which was fourteen, and her father's voice, which was stern. Rateyes thought he had himself a little nymphomaniac, right from the lies his older brother always told him. "I'm workin'," Julia said.

New York is the center of the Empire. The disintegration of the Empire is the fissures that start in New York. Rateyes and I know about this and can get vibrations from a walk down the street anywhere in Manhattan. And at this time, when we found out that the impossible *hadn't* happened, that there *wasn't* a beautiful baby girl on a freezing street in the dead of night who waited and was waiting for love, at this time another finger was stuck in the Jello and the Empire quivered from the center outward, closer than it had ever been to collapse. Rateyes said, "Holy shit, you have to do that, huh?" and nodded like a weak old man. I guess everyone has to do something. Rateyes was very understanding, and he absolved her, as he had only last night absolved a black man who pulled a gun on him in the elevator of his building, by saying, "It's too bad you have to do this to get bread, man. Here. I wish I had more." And then, when this black man had responded to the kindness in Rateyes' face and said he hated holding people up and he hoped he would never have to shoot anyone, but he needed the money for heroin, Rateyes had said, "Look, take care of yourself. You're a good man and it won't be long before we're

[2]

on the same side." Rateyes had left the elevator glowing like danger and pleasure, with the feeling he had made his first contact with the army he would soon come to lead. When he told me about the guy in the elevator there was such a sense of new friendship in the things he said I asked if he had taken the thief's phone number, just in case they ever wanted to get together again.

I thought that the reductions in price of the things in this window were incredible, as incredible as they said they were. I am not interested in prostitutes because I am afraid of disease. Rateyes, on the other hand, has always been interested in prostitutes, but lately he has come to believe that to pay a prostitute for sex is to become a part of the bullshit oppressive hierarchy of exploiters and panderers. He is disgusted with the formal oppression society daily forces us to engage in and he is trying to break out of it whenever he can. He tried to talk her into doing it for free. "Look, do you ever just feel like doing it, you know, without all this money hassle? I mean do you ever just meet a cat and say, 'What the fuck, I'm just gonna *do* it'? I'd like to know." She said no, except for her boyfriend. She said she needed the money for heroin. "I got a habit, wow, you know?" Rateyes knew all right. "Look at that, Elia. Isn't this the center of the fuckin' Empire! Well, how much do you think you would need like to do your thing?"

She said twenty dollars.

Rateyes (pseudonym of respect and affection, referring to the constant laser glow of ratty quick desire in his eyes) stared at her with kindness. "You must have a pretty heavy habit, huh? Shit, they really have ways to fuck you up. . . . They really fuck you up. . . . You need twenty bucks, right?"

Julia was no fourteen and has bargained with every

tone of voice there is on 86th Street. "What about seventeen? Wow, man, I have to have it."

Rateyes shrugs. "Look Elia, do you have seventeen bucks? You know, I was robbed yesterday." We hustled her into a cab and tried to talk to her about some things. We tried to talk to her about the Panthers, Eldridge Cleaver, The Young Lords. She had never heard of any of these things. Right here in the center. Right here. We said, "Look at what they do to them," and we knew what we meant. Even Julia seemed to know what we meant. She said, "Yeah, man, I hate this fuckin' city, man. Wow I wish I was in the country, man. Wow I wish I *was*." This was a very tough night for her. She had been kicked out of her hotel so she didn't have a place to take men.

We took her to 102nd Street, where Rateyes' brother Stewart lives. This is an ugly apartment, with catshit and newspapers all over the floor. Rateyes is crashing here for a couple of weeks and he has put his sleeping bag over a mattress on the floor. There is a pound of grass in the foot of his sleeping bag and Rateyes crawls in after it head first. While he is there in the dark he decides he doesn't want to screw Julia after all. He comes out with a big grin and a fistful of loam. "Look, this is bullshit. We're friends. We don't have to get into this sex thing right in the middle of nothing." Rateyes and I begin to roll joints. We both feel like the just prince. Rateyes and I feel like talking to Julia. There is a disgusting thing that the radical children of the middle class get into when they are left alone with members of the lower classes. This thing you have probably seen or done yourself. In a way, it is pumping for information; in a way it is the baldest condescension. Telling a cab driver in New York it must be tough to drive a cab in New York is one way to do this thing.

[4]

Another way is to use foul language in friendly conversation with a handyman, on the assumption that he is more comfortable with you if you speak like that. We wanted at that time to get into that very thing with Julia. We wanted a glimpse and a closeness in a different world.

Julia, on the other hand, is panicking. We have had moods and our moods change and will change and are changing, but Julia needs twelve dollars immediately so she can score on 116th Street or she will "get sick." No matter what Rateyes or I say to her, she says "You don' wanna fuck? Wow, man." Finally we get it. I give her the money and some for a cab. We ask her to come back. She can fix here. Without her hotel room and not wanting to fix at her mother's house, location is a big problem for her. Or else it is certain she would not return. We are getting very stoned and listening to records and already do not really care if she comes back. We now know that she is twenty-five and has a child who is cared for by her mother, and we can see that while her face and neck above, and her legs below, are young and beautiful, her torso is already sacklike. She scratches a lot, and where she scratches forms of life are set free. However, Rateyes and I are still aware that this is the center of the Empire and we are very stoned and we feel the greatest need to do the greatest good for all prostitutes and drug addicts. We have promised her the moon and freedom, and we do hope she will return to claim these promises, to show us that she values them.

The first thing we have promised her is free dolaphine, which she needs to kick her habit. She is certain she will kick her habit if she can only get some of these and Rateyes says he has a friend who is a doctor.

The second thing we have promised her is a trip to

the country. She is certain she will be able to kick her habit if she is in the country. She has said this. It is the city that bothers her. We will get her a big bucket of dollies and then we'll take a ride to New Hampshire and live for a few days in a cabin which Rateyes and I know of there. She will be our ward. The just princes know how to make you happy. In this way we do wish that she will return, valuing our promises and believing that she will benefit from having met us.

When Julia goes to score, she leaves with us a brown paper bag which contains everything she kept with her in her hotel room: a pair of Arabian slippers, a towel, a toothbrush, soap in a plastic case, and a pair of stockings. While she is gone Rateyes rifles through the bag looking for cigarettes.

She does return. She is already getting sick. She is nervous when she takes her works out of her purse, which is ivory with stitched pink flowers. After that Rateyes and I are alternately staring at her arm and jerking our heads left and right to avoid her arm. We are repulsed by the sight of her hitting up. Her face is as dour as a seamstress. Her arm is muscular with veins like insulated electrical wires. The whole scene is too much like frogs' legs and electric prods for Rateyes and me to watch. Occasionally we look at each other and register amazement. Such a show! Right here in the center, in the center of the center, where we are stoned and catshit smells like the earth, the clean earth. Here among us the real true lives of the real true people are revealed to Rateyes and me, and we are thinking *stick with me and the most amazing amazing things will happen . . . right in front of you. . . .* How are we watching her now? Is it like we watch an accident or a fire? No, this is the way we have watched subtlety and perfection, perfect things being perfect before us and astounding us. That is the way we are watching her.

After the difficulties of finding a vein and keeping her eyedropper from slipping off the rubber-hard cord she wanted to puncture, she carefully replaced her works and made herself comfortable to nod along with the record that was playing. Every now and then her mouth would move as though she were singing along, but she was not singing along. Once she stopped her head from dropping onto the table and once she let it drop to the table. A half hour later she got out of her chair and attempted to dance to a song. When the record stopped she walked to the records lined up on the floor and bent down to find one. Ninety minutes later she had still not found one. She had, in fact, not moved a muscle. Her hands were on a record, her head was down near the floor, her ass was in the air. I said, "Julia, Julia, what are you doing?" She said, "I'm lookin' for a record, man." Then she went to the bathroom and we did not see her for six hours. Rateyes and I left the apartment for something to eat, got some newspapers, came back and read them, dozed off for a little while and woke up. She was still in the bathroom. We didn't know what to do. We giggled in helplessness. Finally, Rateyes' brother Stewart got up and desired to use the bathroom. We didn't say anything, hoping the situation would correct itself. He pushed at the bathroom door but there was something in the way. We told him to push harder. He did. It opened a little and he looked in to see Julia sitting on the toilet. Her eyes were half open and she was looking at a magazine which was spread over her lap. Stewart said, "What the fuck is going on in the fuckin' bathroom?" We told him to try to get her out. Rateyes was pretending to sleep in his sleeping bag. Stewart was getting angry. He threatened to take a piss on her if we didn't get her out of the bathroom. Actually, we had been avoiding the situation these six hours because we suspected that she had died of an overdose, and we wanted to be a little straighter before we decided what to do with the body. Rateyes had said, when we went for breakfast, that we would probably have to leave her on the roof. We couldn't call the police because Stewart's apartment was such a political apartment. A political apartment is one where the occupants feel themselves to be watched by the FBI and suspect that their phone is tapped. "They're just looking for an excuse to bust Stewart."

I went to the bathroom and said, "Hey, Julia. Get up Julia!" She didn't move. Rateyes had his head hidden in his sleeping bag. I reached in through the crack in the door and tapped her on the shoulder. She didn't move. Finally I decided to shake her hard and scream at her. She made startled motions and looked at me angrily. She was offended that the door was open. "Hold it man. Give me a chance to take a shit."

I said, "Julie, you've been in there for six hours."

"No . . . bullshit, man."

"You have. Six hours."

"No . . . bullshit man . . . shit, man." Then I told her we had thought she was dead. She shifted to a dreamy stoned voice. "Yeah? . . . Wow, yeah, that happens to me when I get high, man. My boyfriend he gets *mad,* he don't like me to get so high, man. You find me on the *floor,* man, I don't know I'm there sometimes. Wow, you know, that ever happen to you?"

We would have closed the door while she arranged herself for joining us in the living room, but we were afraid she would nod again. Each of her minutes is like hours in complexity and change, but she can let thousands of them go by without noticing their passing. We took her out of the bathroom and we did not any longer feel the desire to help her. It was the middle of the morning and Rateyes and I wanted to split for downtown, and Stewart had to go to work, and the night was over. What we wanted was for Julia to stay awake. After the bathroom she stiffened twice more, once with her fingers on the zipper of her pants and again in a cold chunk of air from the refrigerator. Rateyes and I tried talking to her to keep her awake. Having no experience with junkies we didn't know if she was acting in the proper and customary manner or if she had OD'd and was on the way to dying. Stewart said we had better get her out of his place and that we must have been crazy to bring her there. "This is a heavy place, man."

I sat down in a chair and Julie sat on my lap, all lumps and folds. She told me again how much she wanted to go to the country. I said I was sure we'd all go out to the country together, probably in a week or ten days. "I hate this fuckin' city, man, it's the city, man, that makes me do this shit." She seemed to be miserable and tired. I knew she was tired in the face of changeless things which she was thinking about. I did not want her to go to sleep, though, in the face of changeless things. I shook my knees and sang in her ear. newyork newyork it's a hell of a town/the bronx is up and the battery's down/the peepul ride in a hole in the ground/newyork newyork is a hell of a town. She liked that very much. She laughed with special glee when I said the people ride in a hole in the ground. I sang the same words again and she laughed more. When I was done the second time her voice trailed softly after like smoke. "Hole in the ground, man, wow . . . shit, wow . . . I did some disc-jockey

[9]

rousers for her: WO MOMMO WO MOMMA IT'S ONE TOWN WO MOMMA GOT TO SAY . . . GOT TO GET IT SAID MOMMA . . ." She was laughing like a girl. Rateyes and I were crazy about her. Rateyes said the city was sure a fucker and he couldn't wait till we all got out next week to spend the winter in the cottage in New Hampshire. "newyork newyork it's a hell of a town the peepul ride in a hole in the ground," Julia tried to sing along, but she was trailing. She was considering each pure word by itself in her mind, going over them slowly alone and grooving on how good they were, especially the part about the hole in the ground.

After that she wanted to fix again, so she got out her works from the purse. Rateyes and I were impatient by that time and nervous about watching her do it again. This time she couldn't find a vein, and seals of blood spread over her forearm below her stocking which was wound tightly there. She was taking too long and Rateyes and I thought this time she might overdose, she had come so close the last time, so we said, "Look, Julia, we got to leave. Why don't you fix out here in the hallway." She was disappointed, but said OK, put her things back into her Campfire-Girl purse, and came out of the apartment with us. Rateyes and I waited for the elevator. Rateyes said Julia would have more privacy if she fixed on a higher floor, so she started up the tile steps. We asked her if she had forgotten anything. She made inventory of her brown paper bag and her pocketbook. "No, I got everything. Thanks. I'm gonna call you about those dollies, OK? When do you think your friend can give them to you?" Rateyes said he'd talk to the doctor today and he should know by tomorrow. He asked her how many she needed. He said he could probably get her a couple of hundred without any trouble. That made her very happy.

[10]

We told her to get ready to go to the country pretty soon. She said, "I will, man. I was lucky to meet you, you know I sure was *lucky*." The elevator came. When it opened I said it smelled like piss inside and I held my nose. Julia laughed. Wow, jesus. . . . She went up the stairs, stained marble steps of an old building, cracked tablets that wobbled when she walked down on them.

Going down in the elevator Rateyes said it was lucky we didn't leave her in the apartment by herself. He said, "Not that she would do anything like, but all they have to do is pick up a phone and in five minutes three friends can be over there, taking out Stewart's stereo, the TV. There's some things in there they could sell." I said that was true.

We didn't have any place to go, so we went into a candy store to have coffee and read the papers. One of the best things there are to do with a friend is to read the papers together and read each other articles. That day there was a lot of bullshit in the papers. Sometimes when Rateyes is confronted with the massive bullshit in the papers he will start shouting, wherever he is, "Cocksuckers! Fuckers!" and he will give the finger to the general mass of newsworthy events and personalities.

We killed an hour in this way, until it was time to go downtown and see a publisher, Bantam Books, to try to get money to do this book about communes. We walked down, talking about how they were trying to fuck us over and how we were going to fuck over them, and about the senselessness of writing a book and also the necessity of writing a book. We weren't clear in our heads about anything, because we were tired and had been tripping a long time. Every now and then, as we went down Broadway and then went east at 57th Street, watching all the models and secretaries go to work, we thought about Julia, and Rateyes kept saying, "Remind me to call that doctor about those dollies," and we considered taking her with us around the country, but after a while we forgot about all that. There were other things on our minds. The people were flooding the streets, cold, tired, dressed up, going to work.

A couple of months later we found out that Julia had called Stewart's two or three times about the dollies, but since he couldn't get hold of us and we had forgotten to tell him what was up, he couldn't help her out.

Didn't I know right from the start how many books there are with these assholes traveling across the country? Starting in New York and going to Berkeley, or starting in Berkeley and going to New York. Hitching, taking buses, walking; boozing, brawling, thrilled, robust, oversized American American men. All getting fucked, all pondering the national character, all rollicking, free, hung up on death and cars, and self-satisfied. . . . Well sure I knew this, and so did Rateyes, and we had no intentions in the world of going across this continent, not even to force ourselves into little encounters with local color, local repression, the American Way of Life, not even for the vistas of America, the visitavision, vistasensational vistadistances of a wide senseless place, full of effort, full of pigs, hippies, roads, trouble, meetings, weather, earth, and bullshit, not even for money. We had a better idea—yes. If you want to know about the USA then read *Life* and look at the pictures. If you want to write a book, then go to a hotel and *do* it. So that is what we did. Two smartasses stealing money, we spent the next week in New York, at the Hotel Albert on 10th Street, in various attempts to create the national commune experience on dark blind tape, humming, glossy, out of our mouths onto the tape. Rateyes would talk, then I would talk, stupidly, fervently, creating American sunshine, American landscapes, mountains, trees, rivers, American men and women, parties, adventures, adding, adding, always adding, data and data, stolen from pamphlets and magazines, made up—like maniacs in deepest dreamy dreamland—to make a *mental* America, a place that was poured from out of ourselves, taped, given existence. Ours.

The room was green, small and comfortable like the inside of an unopened gift. The furniture was painted with light green-flecked paint, the beds were covered with beige poplin spreads, all stained, ripped, soft, moist, and the hotel smelled like a hospital and had signed photos of rock and roll bands that have stayed there and failed, some long ago, some recently (determined from the hairstyles of the groups—before the Beatles, after the Beatles) all preserved above the front desk, over the mailboxes, the way some delicatessens have their pix of comedians. To this place we brought our new pound of grass, five hundred dollars' worth of cocaine, our wholesale-bought tape recorders and blank cassettes, and we made every effort, every effort. Our idea was to finish this book in a week, hold it for a couple of months, bring it back to the publisher and get the rest of the advance. Isn't that grotesque? We interviewed each other. I was us and Rateyes was the young hippie chick; Rateyes was us and I was the guru; I was us and Rateyes was an ex-Green Beret in the Berkeley Hills, teaching his commune how to shoot guns. Didn't I know right from the start that the standardization of even our newest, our purest American humans and their newest, purest ways, has already started, and didn't I know that the spirit of my times, my era, my years, was already dealt out and distributed among a society of born and raised mimics, hippie types, pig types, college types—and don't you know it, too—that the thoughts and feelings that made my generation unique, amazing, for its short time, have already dropped from our minds down to our clothes and out to our possessions—stereos, moccasins, motorcycles—being diluted, lost, in being displayed so much, admired so often, until finally the demand among us for these unique thoughts and feelings became so great that they had to be manufactured as fashions and wallposters, and that now we are dressed in and sitting on and adorned by them—and they are so weak they are gone, these feelings of tremendous confidence energy resistance to America—Well of course I knew that, I could see that, and I had no desire at the start to see this country.

No, all I wanted to do, and all my friend Rateyes had in mind, was to snort this cocaine and sail through the streets of the Village, walking long, fast, puffing, feeling like two important men of the coming revolution. No one knew we were in the city. No one had any idea what we were doing. And this made us feel that we were up to something secret that would have far-reaching consequences and would help to bring down the American Empire. Long walks. Powerful urban monsters, myself and Rateyes. And it was not so strange to me when after a couple of days, for no reason, Rateyes began to slip into doorways and alleys when he saw the police. At first I said, "What the fuck do you think you're doing?" but he would close his eyes and motion me to join him with a jerk of his head, like a man selling stolen watches. "Lookit, Elia," Rateyes said, "the pigs aren't fucking around. The way to look at it, we're in training, you know? The way I look at it, there is no fuckin' reason we should let the pigs know where we are at every moment. They could take us out man. You know? They could decide to just take us out." I agreed. Rateyes was dead right. Because what did we look like, braiding dogwise in and out of the streets, Rateyes and myself, Rateyes a speedy hawkeyed Rasputin, with a nose and black beard reproducing the same bent curve off the surface of his face, with his Indian headband around his hair and forehead, with his triangle suede jacket and romantic muffler, myself a strange giant with a cute big face, long black hair full of filthy corners, knots, a heavy black wool coat coming down like a circular shower curtain around myself, who was motionless top to bottom except for darting booted feet, what did we represent? What did we look like, chain smoking Camels, leaning forward as we went, eyes either dead or huge and wet with drugs, talking, moving our arms, smashing into other people, what were we?

Guerrillas. Rateyes knew it; I knew it. When we got dressed in the morning and we hit the streets, again, again, in daylight, in darkness, we were the representatives wherever we went of the world-wide anarchic impulse. Potential trashers, potential trouble, always almost what we felt ourselves essentially to be, always potential, looking dangerous.

And then back again upstairs with bags of food and soda to the green interior, green tape, creating a mental America with minds full of jaundice and without details, where imaginary runaways are finding homes in this or that commune we made up, and the crops are doing great in one place and another place supports itself with handicrafts, and everyone is sharing, giving, having babies, full of consciousness, full of words, and some places are armed to the teeth and some have gone out on missions, and so on. And there is no difference between this book here—the one I am writing—and those tapes, except that this book is, of course, 100 percent true and those tapes are 100 percent lies. In every other way they are the same. Everything is exactly as you imagine and have always imagined it to be. Everything is exactly as Rateyes and I imagined it to be, also. If you know five people at this time, you are already in possession of enough data to create your own mental America. You need no instructions and you can't be wrong. Armed love in the sniveling metropolis, armed love on the baked plains, armed love in every town and village. And what after all is this thing called Armed Love? It is the condition of total war that exists before advertising breaks down, the condition in which the country has existed for several years now, and it bears the same relation to war that the Golden Years bear to death.

But finally the thought: All these words, all this crap, spun out of two New York heads. And Rateyes and I had to find the actual, the real and physical country, get away from ourselves and our minds that were all around us, reproduced in the objects of the city, sloppy, sloganized, fast, insensitive, useless. And even though I was aware of the formlessness and unsatisfactory mass that so many people have found in this country, I decided there was nothing to do but to go into it, go to the communes, find my friends, and all and only for the purpose of discovering my true community, of course among the proliferated hippies, the freaks of America, of course in the communes and wherever we are collecting ourselves, of course with the hope of changing myself, giving myself up, descending from privacy into a community for which I could feel trust, of course not satisfied with the ways of living and acting in America and looking for a better way. Face the nation . . . get going. And Rateyes and myself, full of all this potential decided to leave the Hotel Albert, leave New York, get going, pack up our tape recorders, buy ourselves some sleeping bags, hiking boots, leather pants, survival books, another pound of grass, and go. The following is essentially a list, place after place, thing after thing, little moment after little moment, abstracted from the eternal unobservable explosive instances of bodies and minds as they move and meet, abstracted so I could list them here, one after the other, in the fullness of their equivalence, none more or less important than the others, only follow-ing one another because they happened in time, se-quence, a list listed, beginning with the story of Julia in New York and ending with the story of Iris in Balti-more, which is not far to go, and in between, as you will see, a series of events that are in an unbelievable way exactly like the first event and the last event in the list. . . .

Baltimore

Here it is freezing cold and we are surrounded by a huge lawn of snow, and a semicircular line of cars and vans are snowed in on the semicircular driveway in front of the house. Rateyes spends the mornings getting dressed, trying on all of his clothes, belts, beads, headbands, wrist binders, sashes, coats, every day and mixing them with articles he finds in rooms throughout the house. We are wasting our time, getting stoned and more stoned, walking every night to the blank highway for chocolate bars, peanuts, Cokes, Fritos, and sandwiches, eating ferociously disgusting quantities of food and falling asleep in front of the TV.

Where we are: This is a mansion that Doug rents in a suburb of Baltimore called Pikesville, where he is living with his brother Dennis, George, somebody named Bruce who gives the impression of being sly at odd scattered moments, Betty's new husband John and her sister Jane, and John's brother Stephen (who has short hair as he is just out of the Navy and feels the others resent his presence), as well as a rotating population of transient crashers, mostly runaways from other suburbs and older visitors, occult and peaceful, from a place called the Heathcote School for Life, which none of them feels qualified to talk about but which all of them say is an incredible place—a commune of mystics and farmers—in Pennsylvania. Of this crowd, never fewer than ten are always in the house, and we spend most of the time in the library, which is large and lined with bookshelves and has cushions spread over a soft carpet, watching the TV and the fireplace. There is always plenty of food, always beer, always grass and hash that Crazy goes out in the morning to get for everyone who comes throughout the day to buy it. Crazy, who has a long, calm face and a thin moustache, and wears a flat-brimmed Spanish hat with little puffballs hanging over his eyes, acts like a sidekick with a full range of sidekick mannerisms. Most of the permanent residents here impress one as being subordinate and peripheral, incapable of independent existence, and, like Crazy, they all seem to take advice and instruction from Doug.

It is Doug whom Rateyes and I have come here to see. He is our old friend Doug, my old roommate Doug, who has grown rich dealing and gathered all these people around him in his magnificent mansion. Rateyes and I have decided to start our travels slowly, piercing the interior with caution, going first to visit our friends, and then maybe *their* friends, and so on, making this a natural, easy trip, in part because we cannot imagine ourselves thrusting, shoving newsmanly into strangers' collectives, getting those scoops, digging for those facts, and in part because we want them all to come with us, all our old friends, and theirs, in buses, cars, a caravan, having a good time, joining ourselves, our rambling group, to the millions of hippie insects crawling and darting through the fur of the Big Ugly Bear, all aimlessly traveling, the great Brownian migration on the coast-to-coast pelt, of the world's largest, newest leisure class.

Doug's room is on the third floor of the house. It is actually two adjacent rooms—an apartment—one of which is covered in purple velvet and has an altar in the middle of the floor. In this room he keeps the shrine to himself: all the photographs taken of him since his childhood, poems he has written, letters to him from various chicks, and the release forms from his two stays

[19]

in mental institutions. The floor is covered with dogshit, because his dog, Zero, is too young to go outside in the cold. And in the center of the floor, on the altar before the shrine, incense is constantly burning in answer to the dogshit.

"Doug," we said, "we are like babies. Neither of us knows how to drive. Now we have to travel around the country seeing all these communes and we will either have to hitch or take planes." We have told him about the book and the money and have offered to cut him in on everything. "Come with us. Drive us. We'll buy the car. Don't you want your name on a book, man?"

"Fuck the book," said Rateyes, "this is a year for doing nothing except getting stoned and getting laid like."

"Fuck getting laid," said Doug, "I get laid right here. I get all the dope I need." But he has said he will think about it. He has been a friend of ours for years, though neither of us has seen him for a long time. He has changed. Looks excellent—handsome, arrogant, sleepy —with his hair very long and thick worn in the manner of Linda Darnell. Being a warlord has done him nothing but good. He observes that he no longer finds it necessary to write poetry because he has personal power over the people and occurrences of his daily life. In fact, having Rateyes and me around, though he says it is good to have someone he can talk to in a normal tone of voice without giving instruction or making complaint, is beginning to get on his nerves. However, there is a chance he will leave with us because he is becoming bored with this place and because the father of one of his little chicks, a colonel in the Air Force, makes daily drunken phone calls threatening his life.

This is a huge, partly furnished mansion they are renting, the shell of a mansion around us like a cave. The people here act toward the house with the bland malevolence of great gods. They are using it up, as though it were packaging. No thought to the extensive life of the house itself. It is incredible and powerful to watch this happen to a house. The windows break one by one from being slammed shut and from rocks; the banisters crack and are left hanging, poised in sections over the stairwell; and there are cigarette burns in the rugs and furniture. One day someone found a hatchet, so there are hatchet designs in the heavy front door and the walls dividing the rooms. Casual, peripheral destructive events in the moments of the tenants. They do not interrupt the flow or halt a moment to note or regret the event, or to worry about the piecemeal destruction of the shell they are in. When it is used up they are going to get another one. Treat all housing as raw shelter. Do not learn to depend on the shell and objects of survival. Realize their destructibility. The beauty of the tenants' attitude is in the purity of the lack of sentimental attachment to their home. Anarchic urban crash pad mentality. Doug feels that once there is developed, either through regulated chores or a sense of permanence, a sort of preservation (ecology) tropism toward one's home and possessions, one is ripe to be governed. He is always ready to leave within a few hours of the decision to leave. He has shown me how his possessions are practically all in a suitcase and ready to go.

You feel in this place the same pure energy of children who are openly ungrateful to their parents, and you feel these housebusters are in open defiance of even the laws of gratitude for comfort and shelter. The thrill of waste and waste and waste in search of the unwastable, the *worthwhile,* absolute *Home.*

This house is aging and coming down. It is ridiculed with supermarket banners and a permanent Grand Opening flag on the portico. It is painted hideously and cheaply. The grounds are gutted and littered with trash and papers. When I woke up on my first morning here I said I must have died and this must be heaven. Today the kitchen table exploded beneath a dance and we destroyed the long benches just out of formal necessity. Most of the furniture has been used in the fireplace. Now there is nowhere to eat in the kitchen, and meals are creeping outward over the three floors of the house. Dishes age and cake beside every bed and chair and along the walls. Cigarettes decomposing in glasses of milk. Whole organisms of reading material—newspapers, comics, books—growing as if from inner life in the living room. The smell of menacing bad food. This is a settlement of transience. A boom town. We are stripping all the value off its ribs.

December 5. We have lain in wait for days now and tomorrow we will go someplace—maybe Heathcote, maybe Washington—to find and join a commune there. The news is about the My Lai Massacre; and they have killed another Black Panther leader, this time in Chicago, and people come through here all the time terrified. A guy named Albert said the Baltimore police stopped his car last night, stuck a rifle in the window and told him to get out. They searched him and his car, roughed him up a little, and left. He doesn't know where to go or what to do. He thinks he is going to die soon. He is small and nervous with yellow skin and long white hair.

He talks about the pigs killing, jaywalkers, litterers, and vagrants.

In the Earl of Sandwich, like an emblem on our day, was a crazy girl. She was thin and blonde with gigantic ticking eyes and chopped hair in tangled shoots. No one in the place could look at her. She was filthy and deranged. Her clothes were torn up and she wore them askew, like a drunk. Soon we were all staring at her. On the table in front of her was a stack of newspapers; her hand and arm were inserted into the stack and she was watching her fingers as they came through on its far side. Grinning, querulous, her head tilted to watch her moving fingers, she presented herself to the five of us somehow as an important woman, a stately figure. I felt this way, and the other four did also. It is something that I have noticed in myself and my friends that we respect insanity and, in a way, admire the insane. "What's the news today?" said Rateyes, to talk to her. "O the nose," she said, "yes I took a nose dive too. And so-o did you. That's why yours is broken and you have spoken." She lowered her head and looked at Rateyes from under the shelf of her brow, raising and lowering the brows pretending to be a judge on the bench. She was slightly contemptuous of us. "No," said Doug, "he said *news,*" though he knew immediately it was not the right thing to say, because it was dull and it suggested the girl had made some error. She was angry. Laughed harshly. "How *many* are we! How *many?*" she demanded. "Let's see. O my! O yes! We're the five dwarfs, ha ha." She was almost screaming, and everyone at the small tight tables in the Earl of Sandwich was watching her. We stared into our plates, not laughing, not looking. We got up to leave, because she had started to make shrill tittering noises that we felt showed her annoyance with us, and as we passed her Crazy said, "You're nuts." She screamed back at him across the restaurant, "That's the nut at the top of *your* penistree!" Then she followed us into the street, crying, her face the opposite mask of what it had been a moment before. "Please," she said, "be simple, honest, and straight. Please be simple, honest, and straight."

"We are," I said. I wanted her to stop crying.

"I'm honest, I *am* honest," she said, crying, harder than before, choking on her tears, as though we had accused her.

"We will be," said Doug, "don't worry about us."

We walked away from this crazy chick, gesturing with our hands as we went for her to calm down and be soothed, stay where she was. She was holding onto all these newspapers. We didn't know why. She followed us a little way, still crying, begging us to do things we didn't understand—not to tell something to somebody, not to go somewhere, not to do something again that we had never done. "She was on her own trip man," said Dennis afterwards with great respect, "her *own* fuckin' trip . . . *per*manently spaced." And that, the way she seemed incredibly and irrevocably stoned, was the thing we could not get over all afternoon.

Tonight we wanted to go find her again. Doug thought he should invite her to the house before they catch her. Rateyes said, "It would be amazing to ask that chick questions about this trip. Like what's going to happen? A head like that like . . . they can really tell you some amazing shit." We drove into the city, went up and down the streets downtown. The only car around. New snow coming down over the old shocked-out sludge. Couldn't find her.

Rateyes is getting a gun pretty soon. I try to stop him, but he is determined. "Look Elia, what do you do when some pig stops you in Alabama and there's nobody on the road and he pulls his piece out? All that pig has to say is you were resisting arrest. That's all he has to say and you're just dead. Just. Dead. You know it happens. Right? You have to be able to blow him away." Indeed, the stories Rateyes reports about the police and the citizens in the South and the West make me feel the need for protection almost as acutely as he does. It becomes more and more apparent that to attempt journalism in the United States right now is as dangerous as war reportage in Asia. Everyone is armed. Everyone is crazy. Everyone is afraid of dying and so many, so many can't wait to die.

Criminality is around here in Pikesville. Rateyes is adamant about his gun. When he was in San Francisco he was riding down the street in the Haight and he saw two Hell's Angels ripping off a hippie. They had the hippie at knife point and they wanted his jacket. It was the middle of the afternoon. Rateyes happened to have in the trunk of his car a shotgun which someone had given him to hold for a couple of days. He stopped the car and ran around back to get his gun, then he appeared beside the open trunk, shotgun at hip level, a cigar in the corner of his mouth, and said, "*Move, motherfuckers.*" According to Rateyes, the eyes of the thugs were open wide and white as baseballs and they ran down the street crouching and dodging in case this maniac should open fire. Rateyes chased them around the corner screaming, "Move! Move, fuckers!" He says there are so many people in this country armed with so many things the only way to assure peace among us is to arm everyone.

"Ask anyone, Elia. What the pigs are really scared of is long-haired freaks with guns. You got a piece and they got a piece and you get respect, you know?" Rateyes is the son of rich parents and there is in his family the instinct for controlling the situation, so Rateyes has probably considered this question at length. He asks me what I intend to do if six rednecks in a Buick stop me in a parking lot and try to squash me against a garage door. "Look, Elia, we're not playing around here. There are some pretty fucked up people roaming around, you know?"

December 6. There is a growing struggle for dominance here between the dope dealers and the holyroller macrobiotic choir children. The latter group has slowly adopted nudity as one of its qualities in the never-ending search for freer freedom and you are in danger of walking into them anywhere, plopping around the hallways of the capacious shell we are in. They come into the bathroom when you're sitting on the toilet, sit themselves on the window sill and start a conversation. Sometimes they will throw open the shades and say, "We're *sun* people you know!" These people who are hung up on their diets are always a little draggy, I have noticed. There is a character named John, a nude Santa Claus who always wears a knit cap with a pompon on it and walks around the house farting, his fingers bunched and exploratory in the depths of a bowl of brown rice he carries with him wherever he goes. He has a benign smile that everyone hates. His ass is astoundingly shockingly immense. All his skin is orange. He has just moved in recently, after an unattended wedding in which he joined himself to a girl who has lived here for quite a while, Betty. Her last old man was a photographer and she's selling all his camera equipment to buy a loom. She does not look too good in the nude—nipples like twin gunshot wounds —so she has modified the canon and she wears a free-hanging shift in her wanderings. Doug says last night he was making love to some chick and in walks John with his cap and his bowl, taps Doug on the shoulder and asks if he can use the record player. Doug says sure. John spends a few minutes looking for a record —the *right* record, finally chooses a good one. While this is happening Doug and his girl are hiding beneath the covers watching him in amazement and dazzled awe. He leaves, the record plays and Doug resumes his ball-ing. Fifteen minutes later the record stops and John comes back to turn it over. Benign smile by candlelight.

There is also the communal question of the dog named Zero. He is a growing baby black mongrel with white feet and a white chest. There are two problems concerning Zero. The first concerns his diet; the second concerns his excretion. Zero is primarily the dog of Doug. A little girl brought him around because her father was going to give him away. Zero sleeps with Doug and Doug feeds Zero. Doug feeds his dog a variegated menu worthy of the dog of the biggest acid dealer in the Baltimore-Washington area; that is to say, hamburger meat, meaty dogfood and chops, and an occasional steak. It is Doug's pleasure and his honor to treat his dog this well, as it is his pleasure and honor to treat everyone he knows as well as he is able. I have known him almost five years. I remember a dog which he and his father had, named Schnops, a dachshund. This dog was the single point of familiarity between Doug and his father. The times when they most loved one another and were least appalled by one another's lives were when they played with Schnops and fed him. For a while, Schnops' back legs were paralyzed and he was fitted with rear wheels, which he dragged around with his front feet. During this time Doug would either visit or call his father every day, although such visits and calls, since they always pivoted on questions of haircuts and hygiene, would leave him in rage and misery. When Schnops died neither Doug nor his father had any idea what to do, what to get to bury him in, where to bury him, and the dog stayed wrapped in blankets in the basement for a week. Then there was a burial and toasts and Doug's father gave him a completely gratuitous five dollars, a thing that was so rare there was crying and almost reconciliation.

The problem is that the half of the household (John, Betty, John's brother who is just back from the Navy, a friend from the Navy, some little girl) is repelled, physically disgusted, by the sight of an animal eating meat. It is bad enough that Doug and his friends eat meat and have blood and the smell of blood on their hands ("You know, man, we've been into good food, *good* food, and your senses get better, you know . . . and we can smell the meat in you, you know. You smell like pigs.") but to slaughter animals to feed a *dog,* an *animal,* that's *too* fucked up. They want the dog to leave the house. Betty says, "Really, man, I'm in the kitchen most of the time, and I'm not kidding, when I come in here and that bowl is around . . . well, you can *smell* it, and there are all these pieces of flesh all over the room."

You have to realize that anyone in America who is into the form of self-fascination that requires constant opulence of attention to be paid to the diet, whether the diet is macrobiotic or entirely composed of raw fruits

[28]

and nuts, is not doing anything other than refining and perfecting the gluttony he grew up with. These particular fat people who at this time could not stand the smell of animal death in their rooms had developed this poignant sensitivity in the space of not more than three weeks. Diet is an inordinately large nuisance recently and it is impossible not to offend. Like the sects of Christianity, the consumers of righteous food know how narrow is the path to good eating. People who only have fruits and nuts as they are found in nature are contemptuous of those who balance the yin and the yang by cooking rice; some people laugh at fish eaters; everybody hates Wonder Bread; and there isn't a soul on a single American commune who could swallow the smallest part of a glass of Coke. ("You know what happens to a tooth when you leave it in a glass of that shit overnight? It disappears. A calf's liver will disintegrate in Coca-Cola in three days.") I look and I am in awe. I look and I say to myself in my private mind: These people look like me; they are my age and they are flaccid and pale, toneless and san-paku; and I *know* them to have eaten Gino's Giants and Tastee Cakes throughout the Wonder Years. When was it that they shot so far ahead of me in intestinal consciousness? I look, I am looking, and I am saying What a lot of crap. Doug feeds Zero hunks of raw and slices of rare and lines the cupboards with Alpo. Betty says she can't *look* at that dog. (Later I will tell you how Zero screwed a police dog during the subsequent drug bust and how this particular dog was thus prevented from discovering any drugs.)

Excretion next. Zero was a puppy and carpeting was general throughout this mansion. Zero did shit equivalently on the equivalent floors of the house. Doug, who is in love with dogs always when he has dogs and who loves Zero, knew it wasn't any good to have that happen, as anyone does who wakes in a moonscape of dogshit with the dog's face beside it on the bedspread. Doug hits the dog with his hands and with newspaper, and he screams at Zero for doing this throughout the house, and he has tossed the dog out the front door midshit on several occasions, on these occasions often screaming also and also often smacking Zero hard.

Understand that while John and Betty did mind that Zero ate, they did not ever express disapproval of the fact that he shat. They had a way of smiling benignly at the stuff when they came across it in the hallways and floors. Dogs will do what dogs do and that is natural. And the key word in some of the most perverse tortuous ideologies for daily living is the word "natural." If it's natural, it's terrific. However, it was pain and a strenuous assault for them when they had to watch Doug smacking at the dog or hear Doug screaming at the dog. ("I'll tell you, man, if you have to act that way, you're no better than *he* is. . . .")

Finally in their hearts the thing happened that happens in all hearts and the daily tug of pity and disgust for the exultant naturalness of the dog Zero got to be too much for them. When this happened there was a meeting of the entire commune in the kitchen and it was suggested that Zero be put to sleep. This meeting looked like the pre-game ceremonies in that archetypal basketball contest in all summer camps between the Shirts and the Skins. On one side of the long wooden table sat five nudes, one with a knit cap, all with small bowls of moist loam to hide their fingertips in; on the other side sat five Sabbath-flashy dressers representing wealth through distribution of drugs and acquisition of stolen property. The second group, in a short time, threatened the lives of the first group. It was said they would be murdered in their beds if they didn't take their mu tea and get out.

"I don't think we have to break up the house, man, because of a dog, man," said John. There was such love in his eyes and he always looked at everyone in the room one at a time when he spoke, a technique of the greatest orators. At the beginning, or almost the beginning, of the meeting, George (clothed, a meat eater, in favor of retaining the dog), a boy who had always lived alone or with, at most, one roommate and who was not adept at the politics of communal interaction, had planted his elbow on the table. His forearm stood straight up and his middle finger rose out of that assemblage and he wiggled it at John. John saw this when his eyes made their benign king's journey through the provinces but he did not mention it. "We never voted on the dog anyway, man. We're supposed to be living together like. I think we should have voted like, on whether we were all *ready* for a dog."

"Look, man, it's *my* fucking dog," said Doug. "He doesn't bother *you* at all."

"But, man, the way I see it is, it's like a crime to keep an animal that eats other animals, see. I mean it's like you're playing God. If Zero was out on his own, like, maybe he would get the food he needed to keep going and maybe he wouldn't. But like that would be up to God. But like *here,* man, here it isn't up to God, like, it's up to you. Dig?" His eyes were love. This is not an accident; in case you know someone whose eyes are love and you don't know why, it is a rhetorical device. It is probably the only rhetorical device which our people have developed (except for verbal diffidence, which is more complex in its working) and its purpose is to allow the opponent to give in. He can look into your eyes after you have slaughtered him with argument and he can say those eyes are love, and it will make him feel this is the time to give in, because he feels you will understand and forgive and there won't be any more argument. If you argue someone down and your eyes say, I just wiped you out, he will never give in, because he will feel himself to be under death siege. I have seen eyes of love work. Allen Ginsberg uses them the best. But John for some reason made you hate him when he looked on you with eyes of love.

"Fuck that shit," said Doug. "Like what kind of pompous crap is that shit, man." On the other side of the table, John was discreetly raising one enormous flank of his body and a dull "puh" came into the room.

"Like I have to *smell* that meat when I come into the kitchen, Doug," said Betty.

"Why don't you leave then, Betty," said Doug. "Look, we were here first anyway," he said. And that is the inception of the conclusion, as you can understand, for any commune. It means, in essence, that communication has not been attained in those areas where it is essential. We were here first. Betty shrugged. "I thought we were all trying to live together. Like I thought that was the idea. I'm just saying we should try to work something out, man. I'm just saying, look, it's obvious Zero doesn't fit *in* with us. We shouldn't be fighting this way. Not if we were together."

Nobody spoke. There was still frustration. Then for some reason she added, "Even like if you were together with *yourself,* man . . ." The implication is that Doug hasn't made a sincere self-examination to determine precisely what is necessary to his life: other people or the dog, the common evident truth of what John is saying or his own blind pride.

People who are not together with themselves in the

world of macrobiotic cooking as written down by George Oshawa, the sickly Japanese who had discovered the miraculous cure for certain death in brown rice and seaweed, these people you can tell right away the minute you see them by their eyes. Their eyes are not together; there is a strip of white below the colored part of the eye and above the lower eyelid. This condition is known as "san-paku." It means your soul and your body are not together, are in different places. You are physically ill or prone to be physically ill pretty quick, and you are undergoing great emotional strain. Doug has already been told he is san-paku, as a matter of fact he hears it daily, and I have seen him privately and in secret examining his eyeballs to try to reduce the chasm between the colored part of his eye and his lower eyelid. Recently he has taken to looking slightly downward all the time to force intersection of pigment and flesh. This leaves him with a strip of white at the top of each eye, but so far no one has said anything about that and it seems to be OK. Not that he believes a word of it, but he has become understandably sensitive to the implication that he is not together.

Five small cups of mu tea are lifted to five mouths in deferential embarrassment for Doug. The nudists realize that Betty has inadvertently (perhaps she was a little cruel, but it *had* to come out) said what they have all been thinking and talking over among themselves: Doug really *isn't* together. Now they are permitting him to bear his shame in private. They avert their eyes.

I had a good dream last night. I went to sleep feeling very comfortable here. One part of the dream was about a family in a car out for a drive. The car was all clear plastic from the front seat forward. In other words, the whole front assembly was transparent. In this car the engine had been moved to the rear, and in its place two small children, a boy and a girl, were crouched and watching the road come through beneath the car. They were both very happy to be where they were, but I knew in a collision they would be helpless. They were in halters, and their father, who drove, shifted their positions with the movement of a sort of stick shift; they were like bomber turrets in the extent and rhythm of their movements. The father was in bathing trunks and seemed to drive the car almost standing up. His wife sat beside him knitting. I remember rubber thongs on his feet as he used the gas and brake pedals. In the back seat, hooked in a chair, was a baby boy. This car went through my dream for a long while. I wondered that I have been having so many dreams lately without myself in them.

I appeared in another part of the dream. I was in Boston, at dawn. Harvard Square. A girl came out of a building in a very short skirt; she wasn't wearing stockings though it was bitter cold. I remember I wished I could see her ass, and then, a little later, I did.

We split. Doug didn't want to come with us. No reasons. Shortly after, got a telephone call the mansion was busted. They showed it on TV, exaggerating the value of the drugs found on the premises, slandering the occupants of the house, indulging in interviews with the DA and arresting officers. There were shots of the DA standing with forty pounds of grass in the basement, lip-smacking smile, palm in repose on the pile like a man with his mackerel. Saw Doug and his brother and George go from a paddy wagon into a building, cuffed and surly. Saw Doug's room, with voice over ("was this the site of wild orgies?"), close-up of burning incense ("hippy-style sacrifices?") jerky, nervous shots of the mattresses around the house, giant flag of Ghana used for a curtain ("the banner of the Viet Cong was found draped over one window . . .") and, as we sat, passive and philosophical, they showed a sheet with blood on it, hypothesized it was the blood of sacrificial animals, and said, "There are many questions the police have *yet* to answer about the house on N . . . Lane!"

Later heard about the raid itself. Front and rear doors exploded like planets bursting in full flight, all the ground floor windows smashed and showed shotguns. It was a joint raid—state and local cops—and also they used it for on-the-job training for a graduating class from the police academy. Only four guys were caught at home, and in conversation with Doug since then he has expressed his suspicions at various times about all who were not present, feeling them to be the informers. The police brought dogs trained to smell out marijuana, but none of them went to the basement, where it was. While the district attorney was posing for the photographers and the valedictorian from the police academy was making formal thanks for a valuable lesson in search and seizure, yelps and small barks were heard from the top floor. Two men sent to investigate . . . snapped out their pistols. In the velvet room found Zero humping one of the dogs. They all got off because the grass was not found in anyone's room, but in the basement, and it was explained that they were each renting a room in the house, therefore not accountable.

I have visited Doug in Baltimore and he is sour, lives alone with some chick, spends his time gazing out the window like an old man. Perpetually two or three deals away from buying a motorcycle and leaving the city, which he says is his goal. He is in the mental state that when he is slightly annoyed with someone he says instantaneously he is going to kill him. We talk to each other on the phone; he is always saying wait a second I think I hear someone sneaking around.

And finally the house. It is not occupied, because in their searching the police completed the gutting of the interior. It is left without banisters, without furnishings, rugless, toilets stuffed. After they moved out, Dennis returned with a truck to remove the light fixtures. The last time anyone visited the place, there was a sculptor living in the carriage house, which is in the large back yard, making shit sculptures out of dogshit and catshit, human shit from the stuffed toilets, parrotshit and batshit, which he fashions into towers and sets up around the lawn. Because of the publicity, stories of incredible orgies and rituals have proliferated, and nobody will buy the house. It is staying ruined, looking good, and tourists drive daily up to the front door, inspecting the destruction and taking pictures of the Grand Opening banners.

The Heathcote School for Life

December 9.

We are cold and alone with our new sleeping bags and survival kits of Johnson's First Aid Cream and gauze bandages that Linda has packed for us, and our tape recorders with which we intend to capture the *actual words* of actual communards, and we are mean to one another in a silent dark house, an old mill. Rateyes keeps saying, "What the fuck am I doing here what the fuck am I doing here." We are reading anthropology books for clues to style. All I have ever written about up to this point have been rallies and riots, but this place, enclosed, eventless, the petty, fraudulent small things of daily life going by, this place is like a faceless dream that makes you tired while you are asleep, and the proper words are not coming to me. We are feeling like a couple of real assholes to be here. The country, country people, sane and relentless.

The school for life is a small farm on the Pennsylvania-Maryland border, population about fifteen in dead of winter, but this swells in the spring to over a hundred with transients and students of the school who come to learn organic farming, receive instruction in yoga and diet, meditation, carpentry. At this time it looks like a small settlement destroyed in the Civil War—a couple of sagging shacks and the main house, which used to be a mill, and an arthritic little stream choked with gray leaves running through the property. Two families are living in trailers set on cinder blocks. The overall impression is of a hideout, legendary Hole-in-the-Wall.

In the main house there was a thick atmosphere of burning mattresses and a coven of people in army jackets huddled around a large fireplace. The room had an overly warm and grimy texture to a new set of sensory receptors. The smell was ripe bananas in a warm mouth, but there was also an undertone of pleasant bread odors. Lots of dust and the sensation of dust-matted things whose dust is raised when someone moves. Outside, the cold cuts through all smells.

There was a dour meeting of the communards to decide if it was all right for Rateyes and me to stay here for three days. Several times we were asked if we were sure we understood that there would be no heat in whatever room they gave us and we'd have to pay a dollar and a quarter for the food fund every day. We did understand this, we said, but we wanted to be there so badly even intensest cold could not dissuade us. We had to take a walk in the pitch black outside, then come back in fifteen minutes for the decision. "You may stay," said Charles, "although it is irregular and one is always wary, in a situation such as the one we are in, of being taken for shall we say an easy touch." Charles is an arch and petulant Englishman with skin that flakes off his face in white coins. He is of normal size but has the face of a midget with a bulging brain cavity. Most of the time he will attempt to act as the spokesman for the group, and when he is interrupted will allow the other to speak, interjecting, "Do tell, do tell," with utter contempt. The others dislike him and at odd moments throughout the evening will say, "Charles, tell us how many light years we are from Mars," or "Does anybody care to tell us the principles of rural anarchy?" and then Charles will go into his act—"I seem to have read somewhere, etc."—with his eyes shut like a man whose face is upturned and succumbing to the spray of a shower.

In the room with the fireplace we ate dinner with our coats on. There is an embroidered doily hanging on the wall. It is like the ones that say *God Bless This House* but it says *No Smoking*. The people here are actually disgusted by the mention of cigarettes, meat, and Coca-Cola. Am coming to realize that what is operating here is an ideology of daily life, wresting the actions of the self from all forms of habit and subjecting them to the will. For this reason every sort of rule or stricture that is rationally arrived at and agreed upon is acceptable to them all. Abstinence from liquor and cigarettes, keeping intake of drugs to a spartan minimum (although they did grow a crop of second generation Acapulco Gold, which they called Heathcote Happiness, and when asked how it was they say, "It was so fine after you smoked it you could go out and work in the garden three or four hours"); and heavy drugs, mind expanders, the everthreatening evergrowing class of chromosome destroyers of course are never thought about. Very worried about our chromosomes, brain cells, and most of all, longevity. Long life comes up several times through dinner. "Nan, eat enough of this, you'll live forever." I am making conversation and listening, with a paper plate of rice and brown liquids, melted glassy vegetables, noting that everyone is completely and absolutely satisfied with his life here at Heathcote. I ask about the crops, but when they answer I am without the knowledge to appreciate the answers. I ask about their relations with the small rural community of which they are a part. There are no relations. Are they hassled by the pigs? No, the pigs don't know they are here. I say, "The pigs do know you're here. They know exactly where everyone is at all times. Right now in Washington in front of a gigantic TV screen one man is turning to another and he is saying, 'They are having dinner, now.' " They say I am giving off "heavy New York vibes."

After dinner Rateyes goes off to make it with a young mother who has been showing off a strained and blood-stained breast throughout dinner as she fed her baby to an obstructive degree before the assembled guests. Rateyes brought Tarot cards with him to the shack where they made it, and he told the future of the baby. She is the wife of the cat who started the commune, a man named Larry, who is at present waiting to be sentenced for draft evasion.

This activity—the stressful studied observation of the lives of others, not as they cross with mine or are affected by mine, but as lives alone, staged close up by fragments, actors—has the effect of making me too aware of the multiple possibilities for living a life now. Different states of mind I see, whole exuberances, each of them complex and difficult to exist within for real people, are at this time for me curious objects seen with the incoherence of a coherent disinterest. Because of the traveling and watching and writing at night on my elbow, I do not know what things can *mean* to people. I see the people steeped in purpose, but I do not know, except in the least way of knowing things, what it is to be inside a life of meaning. Revolution, love or family.

I have always hated traveling. The world makes sure that men who hate traveling will always travel.

It is late at night. All the other rooms have heat. They told us this. On the radio, our friend is quoting the commodity prices from the center of America. Beef is up, pork is up, baby this and suckling that. After the revolution meat will be scarce and cows will once again feel themselves to be beautiful women.

Alex and Diane are back to back, two sacks of potatoes almost falling; they are paranoid together in a scary world. Alex is a silent young black man and Diane is a heavy blonde; they live in a tent away from the main cluster of shacks and trailers that make up Heathcote and they are rarely seen around the place. Often they will come in around dinnertime, but they don't eat with everyone else, because there is a food fund which they cannot afford to contribute to. Instead they bring two bags of nuts and raw fruit. "This is the stuff man originally ate, before he had fire or weapons. It's the best thing in the world for us. We stay pretty high on fruits and nuts. We tried that macrobiotic shit for a while but it brings you down because what you're doing is cooking all the natural truth out of your food," says Alex. Alex and Diane spend their days knitting ski caps out of wool, which they sell at the Heathcote store to people who come looking for organic foods. These hats are their only source of income. They have lived on no money at all for almost six months, since they had to escape Arizona, where they went to school together, because Diane's father threatened Alex's life.

Why are you living here?

See, I can't make it in the city, because you got to pay rent, you can't get food without paying for it, you got to get a job. I don't want to work because whatever work anybody is going to give me got to be shit work. Out here you don't need money.

What do you mean, you only live here because its economically feasible?

Yeah, it's just for the winter, then I think me and Diane'll go out West again. Maybe we'll go to California. I have some people out there we can stay with for awhile. You can't hitch in the winter though.

You like it here?

It's OK. They leave me alone. Charles hates me, I can tell that. But I don't hate him. I wouldn't hurt him, but if he come after me what else is there to do. I wouldn't hurt him, though.

What are you talking about? You mean you have fights with someone here?

Charles turns the others against me and Diane. They don't really care, I guess, but they don't know, so if someone tells them this and this they start treating you like shit. I don't care but I don't feel comfortable. I don't need them though. I got Diane. All the other chicks want to fuck me, and they all know that, but Diane won't fuck the other cats. Maybe that's why they're down on us. I don't know. It doesn't matter.

Is there anyone here you really like?

There's nobody here *nobody* really likes. I think this place is going to split up in the spring. They're not into anything. Just farming and shit, and they're not really into any kind of farming either. So you just sit around and look at each other and say What you do today, and you say, I don't know. I guess I went into town and bought a paper, or I cut some wood or some shit. Pretty soon you start to hate everybody because they're always right there and they got nothing to say.

December 12. We have been here three days and almost everyone has called me aside to talk in private against everyone else here.

Martin does yoga. I told him I had a crick in my neck from sleeping on the freezing floor using shoes for a pillow. He said coffee and nicotine gave me the crick

[42   ]

in my neck and did handstands and other acrobatics in a supermarket to show me what it was like to be in good shape. Then he grabbed my head and cracked my neck. It felt better immediately.

The sex life of Heathcote is very weird. Everyone we have asked says they practice monogamy here, except Alex, who claims to have fucked everyone. At dinner last night, they all outlined the sexual philosophy of the commune, saying the individual family is the core unit of life; husbands and wives, parents and children, traditionally allotted to one another. Said that living so closely with one another, the reverberations of one man or woman changing partners, leaving one or two others loose and therefore on the make, would be too violent and extreme for the place to tolerate. Surprisingly, it was the whole population of the commune telling this, nodding agreement, all in accord. In the three days I have been here it has been apparent that everybody is making it with everybody else and with all visitors. Just a while ago one guy came downstairs from his chick's room on the second floor, ran into his wife who was peeling potatoes in the kitchen, told her he was just back from a day in Baltimore. It would be a mistake to say there is any kind of sexual liberation here, because the enterprise is carried out with sneakiness and no honesty at all. In this way, Heathcote seems to resemble any suburban community where vapid tranquility is hiding vapid turbulence of impropriety. This may be because the natives are not young people—most are almost thirty—and grew up in previous insane periods of sexual fashion. Moving around the place and watching them scurry here and there, on the sly, creating all the nuances and complexities of traditional small society sexpolitics even on this barren freezing farm is as frightening as going out into a storm. We have entered a psychological terrain like an electric storm, full of jealousy, danger, suspicion, intrigue; and these tensions and pressures are somehow thrilling to watch. They are all so close to one another, relentlessly carelessly *there* in front of one another day after day, dinner after dinner, suspecting one another and holding grudges that last incredibly long times and bored with one another, and all these people are like a single obsessed brain. When they talk to me, it is obvious that each thinks of himself *completely* in terms of what the others think of him and how he relates to each one of the others. The place is a microcosm of every form of international terror and paranoia.

And yet, like the poor and ignorant populations of the world, these people have built from the massive negative evidence of their actual lives a real childbirth mystique. None of them wants anything better than to have children. Sue and Ruth are both expecting. This will be Sue's third child. She will give birth in her cottage, with the whole commune around her holding candles and singing Beatles' songs, as she has twice before. Sue says women are very fucked up because they are "not allowed to partake of the peak experiences of womanhood." They are propagandized into believing that childbirth is painful; she says it is orgiastic pleasure. She lost a previous child when it caught pneumonia in a ward of newborns in a hospital—says in Finland and Sweden, where infant mortality is lowest, they have reverted to home births because babies are immune to all the germs in the home of their parents, but not in hospitals.

I will never be in the mood to describe the physical truth of Heathcote because it did not make me feel anything when I looked at it. It was my first stay in the country in a long time and I tried to feel what it was there was to feel about it, but the feeling was only the distance from the world and body that I have felt on the subway in New York. Someone here built a log cabin with his wife, using only a hatchet and a knife. It was beautiful and small and I felt I wanted to take a picture of it, but not really. I wanted to celebrate and there were no celebrations so I loaded myself with dope and I walked into pitch-black cold. I shook my head and it was a panful of grain rolling and rolling, gravelly and solidly moving as a panful of grain. Then I went into the main house where they were leaning like brackets over paper plates having their dinner. I called my friend Doug to come and take Rateyes and me away from Heathcote. In an hour he was there with a carful of people and wine, screaming down the private road past the still trailers to get us. We all drove back smoking dope from a water faucet Doug stole at Woodstock. He asked us what it was like there. He thought we were idiots to sleep on floors with people who didn't eat meat. He distrusts young people with religion. Rateyes said: "The sun sets daily in the roof of her mouth. A tractor drags behind us, pulling up land and secrets." He also was not happy there.

I wondered how I would be able to talk to people who have changed their lives, have chosen lives for themselves that are different from the lives that seemed apparent when they were growing up. I wondered how I could talk to people who were *most* concerned with living a *long time*. Everyone at Heathcote gave as prime reason for each action, each dietary decision, each concern, the fact that whatever it was would prolong his life. He would get to be older. I cannot understand the thrill of longevity.

Washington, D.C.

December 14.
Washington is a city I have never visited but I have marched on it three times. First stop was the luxury apartment of a minister who looked like John Carradine, wore a black suit and minister's collar, high cowboy boots with deeply embossed laughing horse heads, horse shoes, rodeo memories. Bruce, who is some kind of disciple of this man's, took us to his place, introduced us as "two seekers from New York." John Carradine says, "What are you looking for, boys?" He unfolded a scheme for "turning on" big business, which many big companies have already signed up for, paying him large fees. They fly him from place to place and he addresses the regional offices, giving them his turn-on kit—sugar cube, lexicon of hippie lingo, two joints, a record album, a bibliography of background materials for optional reading (*Howl, Siddhartha, The Whole Earth Catalog* and so on) so they will be better equipped to handle sales and marketing directed at the expanding "youth market." "That's the *real* revolution, boys. . . . There's nothing wrong with capitalism except it isn't turned *on*, it isn't tuned *in*." He said he was infiltrating at the very highest levels of industry and government, getting stoned with the prime porkers. Proceeded to get stoned with us on our incredible new grass that makes people weep and laugh and confess things they have never told anyone. After the first joint he was sobbing, clenching his hands on his knees like Lincoln's statue, saying, "Sometimes it all seems so useless, useless, all the smirking faces, all those fat greedy bastards, always the same stupid questions, always the lack of respect. . . ." His eyes flowed freely, widely staring me in the

face, as though he was experiencing clarity of vision for the first time. He was in such instantaneous and engulfing sorrow we told him to cheer up, it was only the grass made it look so bad. In the other room, singing inhumanly, were his wife and a circle of kids who worship him and assemble to hear him rapping incredible "Money Is Psychedelic" speeches. Some of them came in to see what was the matter. He said, "My children, I have come to a fork in the road," sighing, heaving, with the weight of his thoughts. Then he started getting rushes. He rushed off to mimeograph a thousand copies of some quotes by Norman Brown on the subject of money as shit for his monthly mailing to the top executives. Bruce was extremely proud of himself for having been able to introduce us to him. As we all watched him hurry away to mimeograph, lost in the clouds of metaphor that represented the real world to him, Bruce was nodding approvingly, saying, "What did I tell you. He's a very evolved cat."

Rateyes and I spent the day visiting the row houses around Dupont Circle where ten to twenty people live in quasi-familial conjunctions of one kind or another, sharing kitchen and bathrooms, eating together, whatever. They are not "communes" in the sense that there might be implied an ideology of daily life. They are logical outgrowths of the specific environmental data supplied by this particular city. That is, six or seven people can easily rent one of these townhouses for less money than it would cost each one for a small apartment. There is no telling if one of these associations of convenience will eventually assert itself into the lives of the tenants, and if they will approach some level of family or tribal unity. Many people do not even feel this would be a good thing, and in going from place to place I saw that within many of the houses, which are together for no transcendent reason, there is a contrary trend toward fetishistic privacy with everyone retiring to his room after dinner to enjoy his own drugs and his own stereo. These places, not remarkably, are easy to spot by the signs that are on all of their walls, telling what hours the refrigerator may be opened, who has not done the dishes, asking for records to be returned, begging you to keep the bathtub clean, and so on like letters to the editor.

We knocked on a list of doors, all people we did not know, introduced ourselves and told them we were looking for a place to crash. Everyone said we could crash. We left each place, though, after we had talked to the people for a while, saying we would probably be back for the night. Finally we just stayed in the house where we were when we decided to stop going around. These people were a light show, all living together with their equipment. It was a house full of special effects, all cavelike with black walls. Constant sensation of furniture exploding under you, of being under night attack. They are all working for the United States Government, making lots of bread, producing light shows for Congressional parties and dinners, proms for the Congressional children. Like the minister, they are very concerned with "infiltrating" the government through their shows. Told us that sometimes they slip movie clips of Vietnam and harsh battle sounds into the show, and this affects the legislators subliminally. It is hard to know what to feel about this. Do they believe it at all? They didn't appear to be mouthing hypocritical off-hand excuses, but were ardent and confident, a small band of dedicated media freaks, and seemed actually to believe they were on the road to power.

Smoked some of this grass with Arnold, a member of the light show, then we went to an Italian restaurant, where he laughed violently on looking into the passing and adjacent faces of men with their wives, men with their partners, all the families of four, bound and tense, gazing away from one another. He could not stop laughing at them. "All their little games," he said, "can you dig?" He saw everyone to be in an elaborate pose, to be wearing a mask, and that was so ridiculous Arnold couldn't get over it. Only he and I were natural, relaxed, authentic. Simple false clarity is the gift of this grass.

My book is about a process without significant events, like a plague or the way that masses of people change their minds about a thing. The only way it will be written is as a list, an accumulation of places and things, people met, anecdotes of non-events, one after the other from the beginning to the end. In this day's anecdote part, Arnold leans over the table and says in a loud voice, sputtering and laughing, "I used to think I could possibly, possibly, turn into one of them, you know. . . . I used to think anybody could. It's just a way to be, the way they are. Like I could understand where they were at sort of. But *now,* shit, man, that can't happen. I'm like irrevocable. I'm too fucked up. I can't even hypothesize what those people think they're doing. You know what I mean? I'm a complete freak . . . *you're* a complete freak." I am listing these things for this book, an accumulation.

A rainy day. The city distances were hypothetical, fading away down every street, block after block, muggy meaty air like damp outer space, all wet stone and glass, wet beggars, wet police cars sloshing around the corners. We went out early, had steamy tasteless coffee, pale and unapproachable like eyes with glaucoma, walked through some department stores looking at all the bullshit, and I bought more pre-recorded tape cassettes for the recorders. We have concluded we will never feel in the mood to interview anyone. That is such a strange deadlock—the interview—with the machine humming, clicking, the needle quivering with every subtle change in volume, an imitation of someone who is fascinated. But nobody is fascinated. Nothing is happening. People attempting to work out some variety of life they can stand. But I wasn't thinking about any of this when I was walking around. After we went through the department stores, we decided to look at knives and guns. I got a knife in Sunny's Surplus, in part because I am going West soon and I imagine myself skinning rabbits, cleaning fish, building cabins; in part because of a desire to be armed. They had knives on sale from $2.98 to $3.98. Then we went to a house on Q Street, the home of some people we didn't know, because we heard there was a party. This is a fairly large rundown house which was apparently somebody's dreamy downtown home with easy access to the Senate many years ago and is now blown to bits. We got there right after dark and immediately felt comfortable in the second-floor living room. Somebody said he and the rest of the occupants are all moving out soon so we could make whatever calls we had to on the phone. We made calls for two hours. We threw our knives into the wooden floor, comparing Rateyes' with mine, trying to imbed our knives so deeply we wouldn't be able to pull them out. People came through the living room with birthday presents, bottles of wine, preparations for the party. Mostly they are students and peripheral activists from George Washington University. We made them all laugh, the way we were drunkenly bickering and throwing our knives. At that time we didn't know any of these people, but now we have all been tripping together, unified by hours of insane intense fun always bordering on the edge of crisis, always almost too much, and we feel like they are our natural family.

This is essentially a "political" house, which means the people relate to one another mostly in terms of world news. Their daily activities are in response to the activities of the politicians and corporations that rule the world, who are always in the center of their attention, and they think of their lives, and every form of future plan, as lives devoted to the destruction of U.S. imperialism and the establishment of socialism. That is it, boldly stated. After a few hours of introductory talk, during which we all got to know one another by discussing recent political information and the daily news, I felt as I have among a few other groups of radicals, the total absence of despair of people who feel themselves to be in an unambiguous state of war. They showed us pictures of themselves in government pamphlets. The pamphlets were massive green paperbacks about the New Left, and our friends had been photographed leaning out the windows of occupied buildings, carrying banners at the heads of marches, throwing tear gas back at the police, always with their faces showing the greatest concentration, exuberance, joy, always with their faces circled and numbered in white ink with methodical enumeration and listing below each picture and in the index of the volume. The faces were so crazy, each in a white circle beside a white numeral. They said in a couple of months they will be ready to leave D.C., where they are beginning to feel stifled and paranoid from excessive observation, will be getting a bus and going to the Northwest to look for land where they are going to begin "intensive military and political self-education."

We discussed politics all through dinner and the conversation had moments of suspicion and distrust, as it generally does among radicals in the process of determining each other's beliefs on various matters. Then, when discussion was winding itself downward, unsatisfactory, tight, and too many people were coming in the door filling up the large kitchen, all opening the wine and beer they had brought, all becoming introduced, and the girl whose birthday it was had come under the influence of our amazing grass and run out into the street unable to breathe, someone handed out some mescaline. The mescaline was in the form of clear capsules filled with pieces of brown and gray dirt. It was very beautiful, clear and filled with earth, like an ant farm. Besides this stuff, Rateyes and I had a sheet of paper divided into sixty small squares, each square being a single hit of liquid acid, slightly pink to show up on the paper. Rateyes carried the sheet around the kitchen, winking and grinning, telling everyone to lick it. The idea of licking acid off a sheet of notebook paper was funny, and there was laughter as each face disappeared into the page.

We spread all over the house in clusters, waiting for the acid to come on, for me usually a period of nervous anticipation. Never actually expecting it to come on at all, and generally regretting that I am committed to eight or twelve hours of intense experience. Soon the various movements of my arm, taking a cigarette from my mouth, gesturing in arcs in the air, began to leave traces and then trails of color. Everyone was getting more and more energetic, waves of deep emotion swept through the living room as the guy with the mescaline went around grinning and lit up, hugging all his friends, and Rateyes, who had been talking to two Weathermen in leather jackets on the staircase, began to perform strenuous calisthenics hanging from the banister while he told them his amazing, amazing plans. The birthday girl, who was returned from the outside, was vaguely wandering, asking the people she met if this was *mind* acid or *party* acid. She said, "I really don't want any mind acid right now. I really couldn't take it, especially on my birthday." I said it was party acid and she leaned her head against my chest, sighing and speechless in relief. I didn't really know which kind it was. I only hoped it was not the kind that causes me to hallucinate psychedelic abstractions in Day-Glo, moving boring shapes that sometimes come into my head, because that is an effect I have never enjoyed. Then another girl who was sitting near me began to laugh softly and sweetly, and her face became amused and resigned, saying, "I can't believe it, I just remembered I have a dentist appointment tomorrow morning. My mind is fucked, my mind is fucked." She remembered her dentist appointment over and over throughout the night, each time as though for the first time, always surprised it was still there, while everything else was changing around her so fast. It became the invariable constant of the trip, a symbol of time and order, flashing back to us in rooms and the street, in intensest pleasure and lucidity, revealing itself around the corner of every moment, inevitable train wreck, her trip to the dentist. And along with the dentist, another constant was a tremendous red roast beef that somebody brought for the party, dripping, running red over its aluminum foil. When it was first introduced, and the donor put it on the living-room floor to cut slabs off it, everyone started groaning, moaning, disgusted, "It's alive, it's alive. Don't kill it," and it did look alive, robust, in the dark room we were in, so he left it on the floor with a large fork stuck into its side and a knife beside it. As the night wore on, and all the most incredible and different things took place, and all our minds went out to sublimest places, most beautiful thoughts, there was always this roast beef on the floor, meathunk, brooding, to be looked at, sat on, feared.

I was feeling good—speedy—possessing magical powers to make people laugh. And the record player was playing, and I was able to follow all the instruments separately, amazed, amazed, and everybody was stomping in cells of life to the music, with others sitting on the floor here and there among them shouting, yelping. And three chicks were the cheerleaders of the revolution, singing along with the Jefferson Airplane "Tear Down the Walls/Tear Down the Walls" and always putting the needle back at the beginning of that song when the song was over, until people began demanding another song so they put on The Rolling Stones' "Street Fighting Man" and led that cheer for a while. And everyone's eyes were huge and illuminated and we were the invincible astounding sexy revolution come true. And the birthday girl was thrilled, and we were dancing that house down, stomping all over to make it shake, and we were having such a good time feeling strong, strong loving superhuman and at the central truth of living in every way that we felt for that short time as though every victory was already won. And I was laughing like a giant fool in a giant red cave, thinking to myself, look how many there are of us, thinking there were so many we were already everyone.

Then Rateyes, afloat in the room, outlined in white-orange, wearing a beautiful shining beaded headband and a suede coat and his moccasins that he has decorated in Pentel, enormously smiling like a patriarch at the end of a long and reverent life, full of calm and love, saw me while I was laughing and bragging in my part of the room, and he floated toward me like a dream, a dream of meeting a beloved friend in a perfect world, and we were both unspeakably moved on the sight of one another, though we had been close to one another and a little sick of one another for days.

"Elia, this is it. I know this is fuckin' *it*," he said, and I said it looked like that to me too, because it was instantaneously apparent to me that he was talking about omnipotence. I looked around the room and we all did look omnipotent. Then Rateyes turned to the two Weathermen in the leather jackets who had been following him around like muscular bodyguards and said, "OK, do you want to get your people together?" Rateyes, unlike most people, becomes absolutely functional under the influence of drugs. Grass puts other people to sleep and makes them hungry; Rateyes smokes it to speed him up and help him think straight. Acid overcomes most of us, laying us back and doing its things on us. Rateyes becomes like a machine with electricity coursing through it. His head was half turned to these two guys, his eyes were looking at the floor, he was nervously twitching to the music. "We're going upstairs," he said to me, "I think you ought to be there, too." Throughout the rooms I could see people snapping out of the moods they were in, being told there was a meeting like a volunteer fire department, serious, feeling important, answering the call.

Upstairs, Rateyes said, "All right, I want to rap something down to you, because I think we're an amazing group of people—you are—and you're the ones I feel I have to rap this down to." He was using that tone of his that tells you there is some special quality about yourself which makes only you and Rateyes capable of understanding and appreciating certain things, and which gives you such an exalted sense of yourself that after a while there is no possibility of your disagreeing with anything he says because secretly you fear he will discover that you are not the person he thought you were. His tone was businesslike and precise, but his eyes were suffused with understanding as though continually moved by the most heartwarming spectacle, like a high-school girl telling you about Hermann Hesse—tripping like mad, talking incredibly fast, louder and louder and louder, almost crying a couple of times, flashing his arms, one foot thrown over the other then twisted back through it like a rubber leg, cracking the toes of the raised foot in its moccasin, as he does when he is thrilled with ideas, smoking Camels one after the other—impatient, almost furious, when someone interrupts—as he speaks he becomes increased, becomes gigantic in front of us— and I cannot believe it, become disgusted, angry. What he is rapping down is a proposal for these people to establish themselves under his command as a group of anarchist revolutionaries, disturbing the life processes in some target city, say San Francisco, in such a way as to create complete loss of faith in the power of the government and the pigs to regulate events and thereby, as he says, "Create a situation of complete anarchic energy through which we as revolutionaries can effectively move, directing the flow of energy along new channels." And while this is an important and essential topic of consideration I get the feeling he is railroading this roomful of catatonics, all turned to stone in their exaltation, all too stoned to think about anything, watching Rateyes like a movie. Rateyes saying things like, "You mean to tell me Washington, D.C., is connected by three bridges and two highways and that's *all* to the whole fuckin' rest of the *world* and nobody has moved to cut these arteries?" His face becomes a mask of comic amusement. The roomful, though they have all worked for years on the daily difficulties of organizing political resistance in the city, become ashamed and contrite. They cannot imagine why these bridges and highways are still intact. They are glassy-eyed, wiped out, and soon Rateyes has become the only and singular possibility in the world of the future. He is the phrase maker of ideological contingency ("Each of us will travel with a thousand dollars in his boot at all times. It is our duty to make ourselves into perfect weapons.") and these are irresistible phrases. I find myself in reveries with a thousand dollars in my boot at all times, directing the flow of energy along new channels. . . . Soon everyone in the room is completely won over, they are dedicating their lives to this project. Rateyes is gratified and an atmosphere of telethon sentimentality is all around us. "Right on! Right on!" says everyone, raising his arms, clenching fists, everybody's face firm and determined. They filed out of the room, little Rateyes slapping every loyal back until only he and I and the two gargantuan Weathermen, who are loafing around waiting for orders, are there in the room. It is a bedroom, hung with American flags and political posters, and Rateyes is twitching and happy sailing from wall to wall back and forth. Throughout his rap, for punctuation and verification of his thoughts, he had thrown me little lines, like, "Elia and me were talkin' about this just today, right, Elia?" and I had said, "Right," so now he came over hugged me and said, "You really had some interesting things to say man—you were really amazing, yeah—

[58]

didn't you think I was amazing, too?" and when it was put that way, then that gentle true appreciation Rateyes has for himself and for everyone else was upon me and I was having a good time again.

Later went out into the street, strolled a while, then went for a drive with some other people, all singing and sloganizing on a warm dry night glowing and tilted. Smoked phenomenal numbers of cigarettes, which tasted rich and foodlike. We stopped near a park, pulled the car into a black tar parking lot, where there were no other cars, piled out laughing, unfolding, and then Rateyes, who thought this large yellow brick building in front of us was a middle-class apartment house, stalked through the vacant lot, lumpily stamping, broadcasting through curved palms upward to the sky, "We are the dinosaurs." We all sort of followed him, giggling, uncertain. Rateyes was creating what he has called "an intransmutable event," screaming, "Come and greet your brothers, the dine-o-saauurs," but this one was ill-directed, the building being the women's dormitory of all-black Howard University. Lights went on, angry singsong voices at all the windows, plates, newspapers, beer cans hurled at us. Rateyes backed off shrugging, grinning, "Good night. Good night."

Then late at night I was alone with a girl named Iris and we were both impressed by new snow falling and sticking in the street, and the car sounds like giant muffled teeth grinding outside, and the vague cataclysms taking place in the plumbing of the house, and bodies shifting, floors moving, the walls parting at the corners like torn pages, the shapes in the plaster moving like cats' mouths. The light was off, the shades were down, but it was impossible to attain darkness, and

[59]

everything was sharply lit to us, because of the way that acid is like the man with no eyelids. She told me her father works for AP and wherever he is sent a catastrophe occurs. She was in Argentina when Goulart was overthrown, in the Dominican Republic when Johnson sent in the Marines, and in Prague when the Russians invaded Czechoslovakia. After she said this, as the house appeared to be crumbling around us, her presence in the room with me assumed a great and terrifying importance. Then every gesture and attempt to talk seemed false and full of false meaning, like a dreary art movie. To consider the meaning of things, even to an oppressive degree, has always been the quality of myself I am most afraid of, and at this time, with Iris and her history, and with the sounds of the house seeking to come from inside myself and seeming to be intelligible statements from someone to me in tones of voice I could understand, I began to wish I could go to sleep. But sleep was impossible, because of the acid. My eyes were wide open, my heart was beating too fast, cigarettes no longer tasted like food but were thin and metallic, like rusty water entering my lungs. I said I was going to look for some downs to put me to sleep, got up and left the room.

The rest of the house was also dark. There were groups of people here and there, on the stairs, in the living room, talking in low voices. Coming upon them, all people I had been with earlier in the night and trip, was strange and also too much like a film. They all seemed to be talking about heavy and important things. No one had any downs. I stayed in front of the fireplace for a few minutes with two guys who were discussing theories of the destruction of California. They both had long beards and very short hair and kind faces. Watching them, listening to their soft unhurried talk, calmed me down. I walked through the house some more and then went up to the bathroom on the third floor. The door was open slightly. I pushed it open the rest of the way and instantaneously the movie I was in changed from dark to crashing painful white, the shock that dazzling, dirty porcelain always provides on acid. And there, sitting on the toilet, grinning, surrounded by the bodies of dead and dying roaches, was Rateyes, and in his hand was a giant can of Black Flag bug spray. Looked at me and said, "Elia, dig it—Black Flag for anarchy!" and the roaches were staggering across the hexagonal tiles, up the white walls and falling backward silently onto the floor at his feet. I closed the door again; everything was darker and easier to see, and I went back to the room where Iris was, beautiful woman of the revolution, fast asleep, fingers of sunlight from the new day resting on her face and her eyes moving, darting frantically behind their lids.

I looked in the mirror and did not seem to be as ugly as I always seem to be on acid, although there were little hairs like tree stumps all over my face. My hair was divided down the middle, bison pure, divided, wide skulled, pulverizing look, two fisted, thud thud, of equal weight, an eye on either side of a broad white space, and at that time I felt as though I were about to concentrate on myself, which I did not want to do, so I tore myself away from the mirror sat down and began to read magazines and newspapers, and these took me away from myself and as I receded, diminished, all this incredible *information,* all these words and pictures, took my place and soon I was a bottle filled with the news. Iris woke up in twenty minutes, completely refreshed although she had not slept in a day and a half. She smiled and I began to rattle off all the things I had read, some of which she had also read

[61]

and soon we were talking about and repeating and reciting the news to each other as though we were talking about ourselves.

Not much later we went outside with Rateyes and some other people, all of us buzzing and alive after ten- or fifteen-minute naps, running around in an acidhead's subdream of pure new snow and blue early morning into which we put the first signs of ruin, running gashes through snow-mounded carhoods to make snowballs and write slogans. We went in no particular direction down this street, down that street until we were lost. We came to a sort of dawn market with stalls in the streets and amazing foods in somewhat unnatural forms of death. Dead rabbits tied at the feet, dead hens bleeding from the neck into a window and porcelain trays, the entrails of a cow hanging smooth as a head of hair, pansful of brains and decks of purplish lush livers, jars of chicken hearts, trays of pigs' feet, tiers of wide-eyed fish with ice stuffed into their gills. Everything was wet and shining dead life and the way it was decked out, layer on layer, an opera house with the lights coming on over jeweled arms and throats, was beautiful to us. We went into an all-night coffee shop for breakfast, there were six of us, sat in one of the booths, and Iris went across the street to get the morning papers, and splash, it was Charlie Manson.

We were amazed, astounded. We bought every paper, read every story, looked at, studied, every picture. We didn't know what to think. We felt ourselves close to each other, perpetually united through the experience of the past night, now in the center of some perfected climactic moment of time. All these stories were about acid, and everywhere was Manson's picture, with his unbelievable eyes, flashbulb shockish, and there were all the things he had done, and dune buggies mounted

[62]

with guns and eating garbage and a hippie sex-dope-and-murder commune and writing pig with blood on the doors, and what were we to make of it? The things in the paper, about these people who looked and talked like us, and the fact that we were reading them right at this moment, after the night we had spent together, all this assumed that interconnectedness, that story quality, which unrelated events and thoughts assume when you are tripping, and which I do not believe, even now not stoned, is illusory but which is the way the world, an intelligent creature, intends to make itself known to our minds. We wanted to meet him, we wanted to ask him questions. Rateyes read one article aloud while I read another article aloud. Rateyes started writing on a napkin, "The tactics employed by Charles Manson, first hero of the American Revolution in the deserts of the Southwest, bear instructive resemblance to those of Fidel in the Siestre Mountains." Iris was looking at the pictures of him, saying, "Amazing amazing eyes, amazing amazing eyes. . . ."

And on our way back to the house on this first morning of the revelation of Manson to the nation we felt as though it had been our energies, the things we had done all in our different places over the past couple of years, that had prepared the country for this new phenomenon that has entered reality to be known in the papers and magazines by everyone. It was an hour after we had left the house and the snow was already shoe-brown sludge and juice-wet. Plows and bakers' trucks, as working Washington began a day's work on the snow. We had a hard time at first finding our way, but this didn't worry us, and we had an evolving snow-ball fight with shifting untrustworthy sides. At one point we saw that a middle-aged couple was watching us through a wide picture window three stories up

[63]

across the street. They were standing at the window, smiling benevolently, sipping coffee and munching little triangles of toast. They were both happy and comfortable in long bathrobes looking out at a new day. Rateyes made a snowball, shook his fist at the window and gestured to show he was going to throw the snowball at them. The woman looked a little worried but the man laughed, put down his cup and saucer, and pantomimed catching the snowball. Rateyes threw it, and it hit the window splattering white a little above the man's head. Another guy threw one, I threw one, Rateyes threw another one, all slapping into this picture window and sending these people back into the depths of their living room appalled and shaken. We ran away down the street laughing and feeling good, but not really good enough, and Rateyes especially was nervous and seemed to feel trapped in himself, because no action could be as perfect or correct at that moment as being Manson, being where he was and who he was, that stoned.

I was busted in the D.C. Court of General Claims on December 11 at 11 A.M. for carrying what is known as a Concealed Deadly Weapon, a pitch-black twelve-inch bayonet, in my suitcase. I had grudgingly accompanied Iris to court to hear her testimony in the trial of somebody named Leonard, who was charged with stealing a Navy recruiting flag at George Washington University. God bless him. I went in sick as a dog with my heft-sized bottle of Kaopectate anti-diarrhea foul-tasting white juice in my hand and sat outside the courtroom with the witnesses for the defense. Nearby, in this marble hallway, were sitting the witnesses for the prosecution, including one short FBI gentleman who was thin and spare from the waist upward but whose legs were thick formless pillars, making him look like a man constantly struggling to rise out of a block of stone. Everyone was heckling him: sounds of sirens muffled behind palms, a dramatic reading of the quotations of Chairman Mao. Giggling and gagging, the witnesses for the defense were having a terrific time. I was at peace with the FBI because my war was with my bowels, and I swigged Kaopectate from a brown paper bag, waiting for this testimony I didn't want to hear so I could get on a train for New York and go to bed. I happened to open my suitcase to get out my tape recorder and test whether some things I had recorded the day before were OK. The FBI man at that time must have spotted my knife, lying in its case on top of my underwear and socks. He split, silently, a little boy carried away on his behemoth legs. I did not know why. Later, because my bowels were a jungle and I didn't really give a shit about Leonard, I decided to leave and go to Penn Station. At this point Iris reveals herself to be the cosmic force for catastrophe that she is. She physically holds me, to keep me from leaving, saying, "Stay stay, I'll call the station so you don't get there too early." She held onto me until a pleasant court officer came over and told me the judge says no one from the witness area can leave the building. "No," I said, "I'm no witness. I'm sick." He said it didn't matter. The judge *said*. I was enraged and imperious. He was kind and apologetic, and he said he would go back and check with the judge. My Kaopectate menaced the corridor between our eyes. See this? I waited, stalking and grunting like the boor I am, until he came out twenty minutes later and said I could go. Meanwhile, before my eyes (whose perception is dull and helpless) had oozed into the area two cops and they accompanied

Iris and me into the elevator. At the ground floor they handcuffed me and read me a warrant and my rights off a card, and I was in custody. They knew right where to look for the knife. I felt like an idiot that while I was being held there they were working up a warrant and I didn't know and I was falling for such bullshit and not making attempts to throw the knife out a window or something . . . flush it, swallow it, insert it here or there. Iris ran back into the elevator shrieking, "The pigs got Elia, the pigs got Elia," although only a small old lady with a pink sweater and a gold sweater clasp could hear her. I looked from face to face of the particular pigs who did have me and I wished she was not that way. One of them, a big fat man with a child's face, pulled the knife out of the sheath and said, "Didn't anybody tell you this is a no-no, kid?"

They took me to a precinct house area somewhere in the building where they searched me and my suit-cases and where a crowd of swatch-faced creeps stood around yammering about the hippies. "I see you got a girl there, Sarge! Boy, she shore is purty!" When I was arrested I was wearing bell bottoms and a pink shirt with a ruffled front. Handcuffed, with my arms pulled behind my back, I felt like a classic punk. Made the most of this, eyes half closed, head rolled to the side, kept whipping my hair back out of my eyes and this especially pissed off the guys who were standing around. Then I was locked up in a little cell. It happens that before parting from Rateyes that morning he had given me three tabs of acid to hold for him. I forgot about them until the cops started rifling through my passport, where I had put them. They didn't notice them because they were three dots of pink on white blotter paper. In the cell, I thought I should get rid of them, because when they took me to prison they

[66]

would take all my things and have all the time in the world to figure out what everything was and what it meant between us. I tried to flush the paper down the toilet but the toilet didn't flush. There was a crumpled ball of paper then, banking off the sides of the bowl, and I thought of them coming in and looking through it for messages. I fished the ball out of the bowl and thought of swallowing it. Then I thought how could I have thought of swallowing it? I rolled it tighter and stuffed it behind a leg of the cot in the cell.

You go through a lot of policemen on your first day in jail, being arrested, arraigned, booked, fingerprinted, moved from place to place, showered, etc., and every policeman I came into contact with said to me, as I left his custody, "Now I didn't beat you up, did I?" or "I bet you're gonna go and say we kicked the shit out of you." The two arresting officers said they were offended when Iris called them pigs. I apologized. We discussed police brutality, which they swore they had never seen practiced and which they believed to be a product of television sensationalism. They didn't believe I was beaten up at the Chicago Convention, except they would allow that an officer might have defended himself when I attacked him. I was too sick and sad to examine the smaller clues of faces to see if they actually believed the things they were saying, but those are the things they were saying. I said, "You beat me up! You're hurting me, you're killing me!" and they didn't examine the smaller clues of faces to see if I believed what it was I was saying, but that is what I was saying, because I had my Kaopectate confiscated. The danger seemed to be that I would constipate myself to death in despair.

Now it seems less than essential to go through each variation in my short term of imprisonment, although at the time every change of place or situation was such a surprise—that each new situation actually *was* in the world and that men are in each one daily, as a natural consequence of the single moment of arrest, no matter for what, and that yet each situation was not somehow famous, a part of the daily conversation of life-knowledge of every person. I am sure men feel this way when they are for the first time in the boiler rooms of ships.

The basement lockup of the court building, where I was to await bail hearing, was a large room with ten long benches riveted to the linoleum floor. The walls are lined with tan bathroom tiles and the floor is green. The ceiling is green. There are green lines running along the tan walls to be some kind of decoration. This is a big, square space with three walls and a wall of bars. Beyond the bars are two office desks where policemen sit and do crossword puzzles. The whole place smells strongly of piss intersecting with old newspapers. There is an incomplete partition—green with messages scratched in it—beyond which is a row of urinals and toilets. There is a tidal movement of water and bits of toilet paper and substance from under the partition out over the green floor. There are also a lot of ham sandwiches on the floor with cigarettes stubbed out in them. They sell these ham sandwiches to the prisoners, but for some reason no one finishes his sandwich. Everyone just puts it on the floor near him and puts his cigarettes out in it and watches it soak up water from the floor.

When I was first brought to this place I was somewhat

surprised because there weren't any other white people. During my one-day residence in the Washington, D.C. penal system I saw about a thousand prisoners, three of them were white. Sometimes this was frightening to me, but at the end it wasn't.

Then another white man came in and seeing that I was white came over to talk to me. His name was Kevin and he had been arrested while at work in the Department of the Interior for nonsupport of his wife. He was a bccfy man with a catalogue of eye and lip movements that were supposed to indicate either intimacy or secretiveness, as though he was always sizing me up and then deciding it was OK to tell me this next private information, and then sizing me up again and then deciding to tell me more private information. He said, "I don't know how they found me. I really don't understand that, son." I said, "What is the problem?" He said, "It's my wife, see. She's a real cunt, a *real* cunt I'll tell you. She says I don't send her any money. Well, I'll *send* her the money when she lets me have my visiting privileges. I'm supposed to see the kids—that's Tricia and that's Peter"—(shows me two snapshots of kids squinting into the sunshine standing in snow behind a suburban house)—"they're wonderful kids wonderful kids. I get privileges every Sunday and two months in the summer. That's fair. But when I call her up and say I'm taking my privileges she's always got a reason why I can't take them that week. It's simple as that, as I see it. *When* I see the kids, like I'm supposed to, *then* I send her the money." He showed me more pictures, of himself and two showgirls on ice skates. He used to be a professional ice skater, and even in high school he toured all over New York State with these girls. They were all underage, so every time they ran off to tour, their parents and schools would send the police after them. They would always go right back out though, and he says he usually did a full season in those years, hassles and all. I asked him if he ever skated with his wife. "That fat cunt? I'm embarrassed enough just to walk down the street with her. The kids are fat, too. She feeds them all this shit and they don't know any better. Two fat pigs. I'll tell you I hate to watch it happen." Now he is a commercial artist, working for the Department of the Interior, but he says if they attach his salary to pay off his wife he'll quit and go on home relief. He looks around the lockup at all the spades. "I'll tell you, the niggers are doin' it, and they have the right idea, the right idea. Let Uncle Sam worry about where your next meal is comin' from. I'll quit in a minute. I don't have to work to be happy not at all, not to pay my wife and those fat kids."

I waited here for three hours, in extremest discomfort, with nothing to lean against, sink into, or lie down on, balanced on a slat. Court-appointed lawyers stride like lieutenants into the area calling out men's last names before they get up to the bars and meeting the men through the bars and telling them the court has sent them to help out. All the lawyers are white and all the prisoners are black, so it looks like a slave market in negative. A lawyer comes in shouting, "Richardson, Richardson, James Richardson," and three men go up to the bars, James, James, and John Richardson. The lawyer goes back to somewhere to find out which one he is supposed to handle. They don't know anything about anyone's case, because this would be impossible. There is a form statement they are supposed to make, and a form of inquiry, to find out all the necessary information and give the prisoners all the necessary information, but like airline hostesses reading index cards to find out what to announce, they sometimes leave out a line here and there. I never found out the name of my lawyer and he never found out who to locate for bail money. The black prisoners distrust these lawyers for two reasons. The first is that these lawyers do not look rich and these prisoners find it distasteful to be represented by lawyers who are carrying failure wherever they go. You have to remember that many of these prisoners, while they may not have at the moment of arrest a lot of actual cash, are men who have periods of great wealth when they go out and buy those incredible outfits, with leather coats and cashmere sweaters and shirts of shiny yellow and pants of liquid green and boss shoes, and they get their nails manicured, and they don't want some character with a loser's head to try and get them out of this serious mess they are in. The second reason is the opposite reason: it is that the lawyers are paid by the courts, just like the cat who is going to try to convict them. A lot of the men can't understand that. Ambivalence in high places. They figure if the government wants to get them it will get them and of course it is going to pay all its employees to make sure this happens as quickly as possible. They don't imagine that the government is going to pay some employees to get them and some employees to get them off.

In lots we go upstairs to a smaller, ranker, lockup where the toilets are closer to every part of the room and there is a stronger smell of piss. There are slogans on the walls from the days when demonstrators were arrested in bunches. PEACE, POWER TO THE PEOPLE, SMASH THE STATE. A couple of the men in my group are writing Fuck, Fuck you and Shit in the vague abstracted way one doodles on a pad while talking on the phone. There is no use giving anything away. This place is packed. It is a room right outside the courtroom, and they take us out in small groups to have bail set or to do the next step, whatever that is, in each of our cases. Some who are called out of this room don't come back, presumably because they put up bail or because charges were dropped. Others come back and then go back downstairs to the larger lockup to wait for the prison bus to take them to District Central for the night. A lot of people in here know each other pretty well. I am suffering in my intestines and scared into a frozen zombie state, so I don't notice or hear things, but it is apparent that some of these men have been in prison together before or have seen each other at these preliminary hearings on past occasions. Nobody looks too worried. I don't know if they are too worried, or if they are not why they are not, but they don't talk worried. They don't exaggerate or embellish upon their situations. Some of them are talking about thirty days, some of them are talking about five to ten years.

Roomful of black men talking in that rapid auctioneer way which is really a slow drawl. I have long periods where the only thing I catch is, "Shit mo'fuck, shit mo'fuck. . . ."

There is one young cat who is as worried as I am. He is turning a brown mailing envelope in his hands, like a cap, it must be said, and the envelope says VALUABLE COUPON INSIDE! GOOD NEWS FOR YOU! and looks like it came from some electronics school or something. But what he has in there is a motion, handwritten by himself in a handwriting like a monkscribe's: Motion to invalidate Evidence. He was telling someone else about it and I ask him what the story is. First he looks at me like eat shit, but he sees I am neither smiling, nor am I trying to be very friendly, nor am I particularly interested, and this makes him feel like talking to me. He is about my age and he is not like anyone else in the place in that he is terrified he will actually go to jail, *be in prison,* captured. The most incredible thing about prison is how quickly everyone accepts his incarceration, how they all seem to go into this suspended animation time warp, slowing the beat of the heart, breathing slower, talking more calmly, to be a body that is motionless and without power. The sense of taking it and taking it easy is so strong they talk about prison and "on the street" as two equivalent possibilities for daily existence. "Man, I thought you was on the street." "Nah, ahm back, ahm back in." "Yeah, me too." "When you go'n out the street again, you know?" "Ah don' know, two three yeahs. Bout that time." But this kid is freaking out, twirling his envelope with the motion in it, hopping up off his slat and walking along the green walls all around the lockup and then sitting back down and putting his cap up front on his head and down back on his head and telling the other people on the slat he's going to get off. He feels like talking to me because I have a faceless face like no face even if it is pink and I am obviously three minutes from catatonia and so I'm not going to take what he says and give him bullshit sympathy or friendship. I am standing there with my jaw like a bag of apples and grunt, because I have my own problems. He says, "This mah motion man, gonna get me atta heah in a few minutes, 'swat dis is, man." He hands it over to me. "You write this yourself?" "Yeah, man, you got to know how to get along in this place you gonna get fucked. No lawyer gonna do this shit fo' you you don do it yo'self." I read it and he has used amazing legal language. The idea seems to be, though I am incapable of understanding the language, that they obtained evidence in some illegal way and he is appealing his conviction on this technicality. Words like *witnesseth*. "Blows my mind, what happened?" "Nuthin but *shit* happen, man. I'm in this car with mah frien's and the man stop us an he search the car an fine this bag of shit in th glove compahtmen we all got to go to jail. The fuckin glove compahtmen. I'm all a way in th back seat man I'm takin a fuckin ride man don know nothin bout no shit in no fucking glove compahtmen. *I* got to go to jail. Fu-u-ck man, fuck that shit. This motion gon do it, though. That was a illegal search an seizure, an besides that wa'n't my car and I don even know the cat owns that car. Fuck, I'm not gon jail fo that shit, fuck. I work in th post office man. I got to go ta work I can't do all this shit alla time." I am nodding. Meanwhile another man who is sitting nearby is screaming because his wife has just testified it was five weeks since he last held a job, whereas he himself had just before testified to the same judge that he had been working up to three days ago. He can't believe he was crossed that way. He would have gotten out on bail easy if it wasn't for that black bitch. "She bettah *hope* ah don git outta heah t'naght. She bettah *hope* ah mo'fuckin don't. Ah'll break her mo'fuckin haid." He has a straw hat on. He looks clownish and almost old. I think he is some drunk or something, or a vagrant, but later is showing track marks to some other spade and saying he's going to get "sick" pretty soon. Somehow the track marks are everything and give him the appearance of having some ponderous wisdom.

The young guy with the motion goes in to see the judge. I do say good luck and he doesn't seem to mind that. He says good luck to me too. He's got his motion under his arm and his hat is in his hand. About twenty minutes later he is back. He calls me a motherfucker and the judge is a motherfucker. The next group is called. This judge is handling about ten men every twenty minutes.

Somebody asks me what I am here for. They ask if

[74   ]

I was busted for dope. I say no, concealed deadly weapon. I felt like a king when I told them about my knife. They dug me very much then. I told them I was busted in a courtroom with a twelve-inch bayonet. *By* the FBI. *At* a political trial. I suddenly realized that my ridiculous accident, when you looked at it a different way, was the story of a daring, amazing cat, The Man Who Brought His Knife To See That Justice Was Done. Consequently it became a possibility that the judge would not recognize that I am gentle and given to collecting souvenirs and he would say, "HOLY SHIT, this kid could have stabbed a *judge!*" It was along these lines that these men were picturing the scene and they loved it. They were crazy about it! "You crazy man! You so fuckin' crazy!" I accepted this adulation as my due. After a little while, though, somebody asked me why I didn't have a gun. "Cain't do nuthin' but shit with a knife, boy."

While I am talking to these men, the flower of evidence is blooming in my head and it is an ugly flower. I am coming down with reborn diarrhea and the taste of Kaopectate; I wish I was in bed with a woman, some dope and a record player, some comics, a telephone, a Coke, some coke, a piece of chicken, good friends coming by with good news and nothing in my head but the anticipation of a late movie, but I am growing to know in my mind that when the police found this knife I was on Federal property, which turns the one-year misdemeanor into a possible five-year felony; I am growing to know that when the police found this knife it was lying atop not only my underwear and socks, but also on top of that issue of *Life* about Charlie Manson, and this magazine was folded back to the page where it says, in a large headline type, "Charlie always carried a knife wherever he went. 'Folks are really

[75]

scared of being cut up,' he used to say to us." And then I begin to know that not only does all this evidence look bad because it makes me look like a hippie cult murderer, but also there is a notebook in there in that suitcase, and this notebook if I remember it right is just there below the thing about Charlie and the knife, and the last entry in this notebook says something interesting like, "Blah, blah, etc. . . . are saying Charles Manson is crazy, but I'm not so sure he's crazy. Rateyes points out that his tactics resemble Fidel's actions in the Siestres and it occurs to me that if Manson's action had had a different focus while retaining the same structure we would not call him a murderer but a revolutionary, etc. . . ." Then I was in the group that went in to the courtroom. This room was ugly blond wood and everybody in it felt bad. This was apparent the minute you walked in. Everybody was either bored (lawyers and officers of the court) or terrified (defendants). With the exception of the judge who was digging the shit out of it. He was a youngish lump of dough in flowing streamers of black and he sat behind a high wide blond desk like the prow of a destroyer laying his hands on big tablet books with pages and pages of punishments. An officer of the court would call out someone's name and the lawyer assigned to that name would step up to the bar. Then the judge (I can't tell you how much this man loved being the judge. I did not add this to him; this was *the* thing about him. It was his first quality and the prow at the prow of the prow.) reads the defendant's name and says to the officer of the court, "Well, what is it Jimmy is here for?" He used everyone's first name except mine. I don't interpret those things in people's minds, but I imagine it was that because contemptible as I was (and I *was:* sickly unshaven, in a pink shirt and my bellbottoms with a tear in them between the pocket and the zipper and little leg hairs peeking out, and I had a Yippie button) contemptible as I was, I was at least white. He called me *Mr.* Katz. This character spoke through a microphone. Nobody else had a microphone although a microphone would have done me a lot of good, and it would have done my lawyer even more good, because he was a pitifully poor projector and I don't think the judge heard him when he asked for things for me. After the judge said something with his microphone, his last syllable would echo for a while, into the lawyer's talking, and I don't think this judge could hear what anybody said. "Well, what are you here for, Jimmy? Haven't we seen you here before the bench on several previous occasions?" "Yessuh, you honor I been gettin' in some trouble, suh." "I see, I see. Well, what *are* we going to do with you?"

When my turn came the problem was bail, and right before he talked to me, the judge had a visit from the judge who was judging the case I had originally come to this building to watch. He whispered into the judge's ear. I said this is too much. The death penalty. With whatever information supplied by this other judge my judge decided I would not come back to Washington for my trial unless my bail was $500. That is, not one-tenth of $500, as is sometimes possible, but the whole thing, and to be paid by myself, because no bailbondsman would handle someone who didn't live in D.C. My lawyer told the judge the whole thing was a mistake and would probably be dropped and I didn't have all that money. "This boy realizes that if he fails to appear on the date of his trial he will have exposed himself to arrest on a bench warrant and I'm convinced he is a responsible young man, your honor, and oopa oopa . . . ." But the judge said, "What are we to do, what can we do," and he wouldn't lower it. I had friends in the courtroom and I turned around to mug at them, because that is the way one is when one's friends are there. They gave me the Peace sign and the Right On! and they winked. I winked and gave a little fist down around my waist, a tiny Right On! It was a pantomime of exultation in defeat and it made me feel much better. They had heard the bail and they filed right out to go find the money.

When I was taken back to the little lockup to await transportation to the big lockup and then the bus to prison for the night, I saw that the relationship between myself and the spades there had changed. Before, taking it for granted I would go free on bail and they would never see me again, because I was white, they had not paid a great deal of attention to me. That is, they may have paid a great deal of attention to me but they didn't touch me. That is the important thing, as it turns out. However, when they saw me come back into the lockup, miserable and terrified because I didn't think bail was going to be gotten up, there were some among them who dared to hope that I would go to prison with them that night. This was about three of the spades. The rest were either sympathetic to them or to me or hated everyone, but these three spades (one fat-faced hulking teenager with gold teeth in the front of his mouth, one guy who seemed to be about thirty, sardonic and weird, and one who is a blur in my mind now), these three spades. . . . "No bail, mo'fucker? Hey, Jesus, you don look too good. You ought see a doctoh fo' it. Hey, Jesus, you eveh been? You eveh been prison? Eveh been fucked up de ass?" I looked at the floor and smoked a cigarette. There are a lot of black people who do not like hippies. There are several reasons for this, none of which is the slightest surprise or interest, although when hippies find out that this is true they are invariably surprised and interested. "But *why,*" each hippie will say, each in his own private time and in his own place of initiation, in his own private blood on the occasion of his own personalized kick in the nuts, "Why? We're the ones they should love. Because we love them. Mmm. A big kiss. Don't we love these black men and women?" And each hippie will indulge himself in a private revue of his past glittering performance in the field of human rights, civil liberties, understanding between the races. Has it all come to this, to have my ears twisted and be mugged for a quarter in my own hallway? Likewise, I have felt this way on several occasions. On these occasions I have first tried to reconcile the senseless insensitive actions of whatever particular black thugs with my own bright past and then, after I have found that I was right and there is not any possible fault within me for which they could be justly working on me, I have concluded, "Fuck the niggers. Fuck 'em." This is the invariable process as it occurs within me. The first time it happened was during a riot in Baltimore. I had decided to go down to the riot area to cheer the rioters on and take pleasure in their acquisitions. I was in a jeep with my friend George and we were heading for a fire which was destroying a Chicken Delight when a crowd came at us with fruits and vegetables that they smashed against our windows. They told us to get the fuck away. We did turn around and we were going back to the suburbs to watch the riots on TV when a sniper opened up on us from a roof. He put a couple of holes in George's window. We spent the rest of the ride blubbering indignant. Fuck those fuckin' spades.

At this time, in the lockup, I was marveling at the chasm, enormous and windy, between the high thoughts that were in my brain and the thoughts that were in the brains of these spades. "We gon spread yo cheeks,

Jesus, don yo worry now, boy, we gon take *good* care you tonight. . . ." Fuck these fuckin' niggers. Balletic beatings stood hard and fast in my brain's center. I became disproportionately scared. My bail hadn't come in by six o'clock and they took us to the prison bus. These three guys had gotten off me by that time and they were talking about something else.

If I hadn't stayed scared for such a long time I would have enjoyed the time I spent in prison. As it turned out, after the bus ride, and after admission into the prison, which I spent doubled over with stomach cramps, I decided to get myself together and combat the inevitable with politicking. I started talking to one guy and I asked him if he thought I'd get the shit kicked out of me because I was white. He thought that was pretty funny. "You sit aroun' like that you sho will! You look like a fagot. You jes asking fo' it like." I looked around and a lot of men were laughing about that. They said if somebody tried to beat me up just to fight back. It seems that if you fight back that generally assures they will leave you alone after that. This made me feel good, because I didn't mind having a good prison fight. Then I realized I also didn't mind prison. Nobody there really minded prison. This is *"NOWHERE TO GO."* A community of congenial souls. And here I am looking for communes! You would think that the search for communal existence would be the search for some quality of life far away from prison life, but actually the opposite is true. The opposite. This is a family of strict master-slave, daddy-baby, fucker-fuckee relationships but within the hierarchies everyone has a place and a definition. After I was at ease, and we were all waiting to take showers, I did a stand-up night-club routine about how I was busted. This was great. They loved it. They asked me about communes. I told them how many times you get laid on communes. There was slapping of palms and the giving of five all around.

The prison was like a big steaming laundry, full of the smell of warm convict uniforms and bedrolls. Many of the men knew each other, being frequent repeaters and happy to see one another. They were pretty certain I'd get off because I am white, but most of the men didn't feel bad about that. You use whatever you have to make things go better for yourself. I think that despite what is generally thought to be the case, the men in prison have minimal self-protective wisdom. They always get caught, and when they get caught it is for something it was not really worth doing anyway, and after they get caught they invariably get screwed to the wall and after the screwing is over they invariably go out and do a repeat of the exact thing for which they got caught. Most of the guys I met were in for repeats of the *same* crime. Armed robbery armed robbery armed robbery, or shoplifting shoplifting shoplifting, or assault assault, which is incredible because if a guy can't get away with it the first time what is it that makes him feel like such an expert he can get away with it the second time?

I got a blue prison uniform and they hung a lead number around my neck to take my mug shots. I was issued a bedroll and towel, a toothbrush and complimentary tube of Ipana. Then I sat dully and still on a bench waiting for a cell and dinner. A little after midnight, after fourteen hours in the penal system of Washington, D.C., they said my bail had been paid and I could leave. I changed back into my street clothes, got a paper bag full of my money, handkerchiefs and Kaopectate, made a contribution to the prison chocolate fund, said to be for the people I knew who were still waiting for dinner, and went out to where my friends were waiting with a car. Immediately on leaving the prison grounds somebody lit a joint. I said, "Holy shit, put that away!" They said, "Relax, relax. You can't let them scare you like that." I thought that was good thinking and we passed the joint around and these chicks in the car started singing their song of the Jefferson Airplane which was "Tear down the walls! Tear down the walls! Up against the wall! Up against the wall, motherfucker!" Cheerleaders of the revolution. Cheering me up.

I went back to the house where I was staying to collect my things. Spent some time telling everyone about prison where in fact they had all been at one time or another for drugs, politics, or shoplifting. We all began to brag about our experiences in jails and prisons, and this led inevitably to a talk about mental institutions. Most of my friends had also been in mental institutions, especially the chicks. Mental institutions are rapidly replacing corporal punishment as the final resort of exasperated parents and in advanced homes chicks who make love or smoke grass are often committed. Except for the matter of involuntary incarceration almost everyone seemed to have enjoyed his or her stay in a prison or mental institution and had formed lasting friendships while there. These places are the true inspirations for the communes we are now all beginning to form except that they are without sex, and as the communes are also becoming asexual, there is not so much difference at all.

I had all my things together but I couldn't find Rateyes to say good-bye. No one knew where he was. We looked all over the house, finding pieces of his outfits here and there. Finally I opened the door of a small closet room beneath the stairs and a cat shot out, and Rateyes was asleep, curled up on a small cot in the room. I woke him up and told him I was leaving for Pikesville to visit with Linda and then New York to see if someone could help get my charges dropped. He said, "What time is it?" I said, "Four in the morning, sorry to wake you." He became annoyed, as he always does when it is suggested that he sleeps. He said he is going to Berkeley as soon as he can get a ride, and then he is going to find Manson and interview him.

Rateyes has decided he must see Manson. We are tired of traveling together. We have failed to collect our caravan. Rateyes needs California, and the strain of his apocalyptic dreams is beginning to tire him out, always expecting it, feeling it . . . *any moment, any second* . . . and nothing occurring; the country is still standing, impure and impossible, in smug armed love while Rateyes can't bear the waiting. He said, "Take these," and pulled one of his bead necklaces over his head and handed it to me. "They mean a lot to me and I want you to have them." I said, "What do they mean to you?" and we both started laughing, because try as we might we are not yet at the point where any ritual can have meaning to us. I said, "Wait a minute," and fished around until I found a nail clipper which I presented to him ceremoniously.

More and more the image of bragging in prison seems appropriate to much of the actions of myself and my friends. Today in a demonstration in Foley Square for the Black Panther 21, who are accused of conspiring to blow up Macy's and Gimbels and the New York subway system, some black kid said: "The pig is scared—dig it —the pig can't do nothin' to yuh. He runnin', he on the run." This was sweet and it stirred me in my armchair. But it is bragging in prison. The boy was young. His face was round, his teeth were good. He wore a floppy hat with slogan buttons all over. His face and the poem of his life are now affixed to the myriad itchy eyeballs of the Justice Department and I pray I will not see his bed in the news all sad and sprayed with his blood.

On the Penn Central Railroad late train from Baltimore to New York I was riding home. In Philadelphia at 12:45 a crowd boarded the train. I looked up from the folds of my sweater, as I always do when the population of a railroad car changes, to watch whatever new chicks might board, and so on. At this time several amazing chicks did get on the train. Two were small gorgeous black girls who were friends and who seemed to be dancers. A third was a mammoth girl in a pea jacket and faded, shredded, stretched-to-bursting jeans. She sat down one row ahead of me on the opposite side of the train and turned sideways in her seat to flirt with me. She was, even through the veil of affection I have thrown over her memory, an ugly chick. Her hair, which gave the impression of filthy hair but which does not necessarily have to have been filthy, was oily brown and dipped at the sides of her face, outward flipped like the hands of Oriental goddesses. Her face was milkshake thick, milkshake white, and foaming with acne, new white bumps and red aborted wounds. She smiled at me and I smiled at her. I thought she was tripping then I amended to speeding because of the lustrous intensity of her eyes. She beckoned for me to sit next to her. I didn't hesitate. I knew we would have a conversation about her life.

But when I was next to her it seemed to me I couldn't look at her. I looked ahead of me while I introduced myself and I looked around the train when I took one of her cigarettes. I said this has got to stop and soon I was looking almost straight at her. After fitful avoidances, evasions, and thoughts of leaving for another car (I do not know and cannot figure out why physical unattractiveness is so unattractive. Did I give a shit how she looked? It was only a few of her gestures—flicking the dips of her hair in a seductive abandoned manner— that made me see, between the spaces of air that joined our eyes, little cooties flying off her scalp at me. She also picked lint off her bosom shelf, all around the pasty spatula revealed by her V-neck sweater.) we got down to some heavy rapping. She was just out of jail, coincidentally, and coincidentally it was for a concealed deadly weapon, just like me. They had picked her up for shoplifting and found a decorative blade in her purse. She was carrying it because it looked like a fish. They threatened to send her away for a couple of years, but she decided to help them with the name of one of her acquaintances and now he is serving five to ten in a Pennsylvania state penitentiary. She was given fifteen days on a farm where, it seems, she enjoyed herself. "I didn't mind it there. There were many sensitive people there. We had many important discussions at night."

Last year her boyfriend died in Vietnam. She is not political by any means but connects oppression to drug busts and the presence of cops at rock-and-roll concerts. She is twenty years old, a fact she refers to often, apparently desiring for me to say she seems older. Why is she going to New York?

Well, see, when she was down in Florida to visit her mother, who worked as a waitress in the Eden Roc and who was dying of cancer in a hospital (I forgot to ask if that process had been completed). Some friends of

[85   ]

hers, speed freaks whom she had allowed to crash in her apartment while she was gone, had ripped off everything she owned and ransacked the place in search of three hundred dollars' worth of crystal meth. My own mouth, even in the present, waters. Who can blame even the best of pals? She agreed and said she didn't hold it against them. She knew how it was and all, especially in the winter. Did they get it? "No," she said, "because I kept it on me when I left." She had been going with one of the friends, Billy. Billy was a beautiful boy. "He really is a very beautiful boy. He's so quiet. Sometimes you don't even know if he hears you talking to him. He's a writer." In my mind I am getting the picture of another freeloader surviving among friends on the strength of a future occupation. Anybody asks me what I do, I always say I write. Oh really, can I see something you've written? Sure, I'll show you some poems some time. Some people say they are drummers and I know they are not such drummers, so it's all right. Anyway, Billy was a writer. Into her wall he had carved "Merry Christmas, Karen" and disappeared into the Philadelphia drug subculture. It was the only writing he had ever shown her. "I tried to find him to tell him I forgive him," said Karen, "but no one knew where he was. My friend Alex said he thought maybe he went to Europe." I didn't tell her Billy was in Alex's closet, with his hands over his mouth. "He always said he was going to England like. To meet the Rolling Stones."

Because of this sweeping ripoff, Karen was unable to return to her job as a waitress on some highway, having no uniforms or even any decent clothes. The things she was wearing, plus the contents of a Macy's bag, comprise her possessions. She had found it necessary, therefore, to sell her crystal meth, pay off some debts.

(This I don't understand, since she was already on her way out of the city. And when I brought it to her attention, she did not understand it either. She was embarrassed. I couldn't tell if this was because she had paid money needlessly or because her whole story was bullshit and she thought I had begun to suspect it was bullshit and I was trying to catch her on details.) And she got a ticket for New York.

When I met her, and it was freezing outside and the train was pushing up into the North and snow, she had ten dollars and knew no one in New York. She showed me a small notebook, the size of a wallet, which she had just bought to use as a diary. The first entry said, "I hope I meet the man for *me* as soon as I get off the train!" I reflected as to how she was taking a tremendous chance. We were familiar with each other's astrological signs and she said our signs got along well. Chafing at my wrists and neck made dozing off impossible. "What are you going to do if you don't meet anyone for a while? It might take some time."

She said, "Good things always happen to me in New York. I've never been busted in New York for one, and I used to live there when my father was alive for another." That sounded good enough to warrant entering the city alone in the winter with ten dollars, no friends, no drugs and nothing personally negotiable at all. I sent her into the bathroom with a joint; then a few minutes later I went over to the bathroom. She handed me half the joint and returned to the seats. When I returned to the seats she made a delicate fluttering motion with her hands around her head, a pantomime of being happy and stoned. She was smiling very sweetly.

I said, "Do you speed a lot?" She said, "Yes, all the time. I'm on a diet. I shoot it." I was stoned and disproportion hits hardest when you are stoned. I laughed. This turned her on to the fact that she was doing hard drugs to lose weight and she laughed too. I said, "But wouldn't your face clear up if you stopped the speed?" (I know from experience that the threat of acne is more impressive than the threat of death when the question of drugs is raised.) She said, "Yes, I used to have a perfect complexion. Really really *smooth* like. But I weighed three hundred fifty pounds. Now I weigh two hundred fifty and I'm still losing."

When you are on a train at night the best thing to do is to go to the rear car and open the door and watch the lights and crossties shoot shoot out behind you, from periphery to center, from big to small to invisible. We did this, Karen and I. The wind was thrilling all over our faces. Still losing still losing still losing still losing, down and down down and losing. I met this chick (I knew this thing inside a wheel rhythm, the way you can know things when you insert them in the clack of the wheel rhythms and you can know them better if the lights and crossties are shooting backward out and disappearing), I met this chick at the halfway point in her life, weight loss and degeneration barreling down the stretch neck and neck. She will either die or she will become a *New York Times* model, and she *won't* become a *New York Times* model.

Conversation was not so much any more when we got back to our seats. She had never heard of the Democratic Convention in Chicago. I wrote in her book, "Good Luck, Karen! You will have a banner year!" We split the joints I had. We left Penn Station together and walked over to the IND. I got on the uptown platform and she got on the downtown side, because she was going to the Village, where her chances would be best, we had decided.

Traveling

April 7.

Leaving New York is a place in itself, which is not New York and not any other place either. Have seen friends in the past for months expecting to leave the next day or any day now, never understanding why they didn't just split. They can never say, because they don't know. Money runs out too fast, people's plans change, the weather gets worse, the weather gets better, you don't feel good, you expect just two more days among all these people and a chance encounter will put you with a beautiful woman who will want to leave New York, too. But if it does, her plans will change, she will not feel good, she will feel too good, and finally she will be unable to leave the city. I have been completely ready to leave since November, to go West and see geography, or whatever there is, but in all little fits and bursts have never been more than a few hundred miles away, and always for this or that reason find myself back in New York. Calling tired friends to say I am about to leave. These friends, some of whom are also trying to go somewhere, are often furious that I might get out of the city first and are always relieved when I do not make it.

I go to Army surplus stores for all that sturdy gear which is so ugly. Browsing in orange dacron backpack areas and among other woodsman crap, overheard two tent salesmen whispering in the aisles about how the surplus places play one salesman off against the other, seeming to be very bitter. One was showing the other the holes under the arm of a plastic raincoat, and the other peered into the holes, blew air through them. Both were appalled about something.

The chance overlapping of purposes says I go with Miss Augusta Holbein, my friend Franz who is a photographer and unhappy Frieda, his old lady, whom he asked me if he should marry, and who was very jealous of Franz. On Wednesday, April 8, my notebook shows the entry: "Still trying to leave NY" followed by this record of a dream, which I took to be my prejourney dream: "The dream of the woman's face upturned on a plate. I sliced from the chin upward, eating blandly, until all below the upper lip was gone. Then I noticed the abyss below the upper lip, then the eyes, widestaring, then that I was eating the face of a woman. I woke terrified." But this was not my prejourney dream because on the eighth, unforeseeably, we did not leave. Franz and I got a Cadillac hearse from a drive-away company and we were almost ready to take it across the country when someone at a gas station said we could not trust the tires. Franz and I called California, where the hearse was supposed to go, asked for authorization to buy new tires, did not receive authorization, and then returned it to the parking lot on 8th Avenue where we got it. While we were in that hearse, though, we felt proud, Franz that he could drive it and I that I could lie in the back in a long pit with a red carpet. But this day was shot and it was unbelievable we were not out of the city. We indulged in anger, self-pity, and querulous irony and never talked of the coming journey with pleasure.

Miss Augusta didn't want to pay for any of the gas. She said she would pay for her own food, but not for the gas. Money was an important issue and a lively concern throughout our journey together. In many communal associations of people this is so. Franz, who is exactingly and excessively fair in all money dealings, explained that it has always been difficult for him to be generous, though he sometimes wants to be generous and, further, does not care at all about money or material possessions. He said the trouble has always been that he is afraid the beneficiary of his generosity will think Franz is a sucker and feel he has ripped Franz off. Sometimes Franz will pay for someone's coffee and talk in this vein at length so the person who got the free coffee will know he did not get it by craft but because of Franz's generosity. Franz knows he is acting this way and feels ashamed when he does so, because he knows how it embarrasses everyone. It is for this reason, and not because he is ungenerous, that Franz never offers to pay for anything he has not consumed.

Miss Augusta and myself were very close for a couple of days, and that is to say, we took up, we left off, and during this short time she decided to travel West with me. Now we are only trouble to each other but she wants to go anyway, to get away from all these friends she seems to have in New York, who call her up all the time and whose attention weighs her down heavily with responsibility, as though she had a family here whose expectations were unreasonable. Miss Augusta, whom I am calling Miss Augusta to reflect delicacy and distance, said, "None of my friends know I have a cent. They'd die if they found out. I'm saving to go to Africa some day." She and Franz often argued about money and methods of saving. Their first argument was about the matter of Miss Augusta's share in the expenses, and finally Franz convinced her she could not come unless she paid for a third of the gas bills. Miss Augusta wanted to save that money to buy presents when she got to California and said that if Franz and his old lady Frieda only paid one share then she and I should only pay one share, and since Franz was paying Frieda's share of their share I should pay Miss Augusta's share of our share. But she and I were not together, I felt, in that sense, and we all knew she was expecting a lot of money from a lawsuit because she always talked about it, and Franz finally did convince her.

April 10. We left New York at rush hour, stuffed in a road of commuters until six, when they had all banked off to their individual New Jersey communities and we had a red road to ourselves. On a long drive with other people. Sometimes their three specific voice patterns and my own seem to be meshed elements of a song; sometimes all our voices are unwelcome and noisy. Miss Augusta tries to draw all conversation on an inward spiral toward its intensest potential—the plane of the madwoman waiting inside her—where all things are actually understood. She is never content to leave a conversation at the level of momentary time fill, and anyone's chance remarks may fascinate her to the point of having her develop them in a drowsy but intense monotone and then come to some important conclusion about whoever spoke. This makes everyone nervous and hesitant in his speech. In a sentence she will have corraled us all into a dark frame. That is the definition and area of her comfort, the delicate (to the point of being insane) nuances of analysis.

Miss Augusta's mood sometimes changes and she is anxious to show that things fill her with girlish wonder. Franz said the evening sky was beautiful, and Miss Augusta said, "O the sky! The red-orange yawning sky! A book of skies . . . book of Skies . . . wadbook of wads, indefinite and soothing massive book. . . ."

"That's pretty heavy," said Franz, who was driving.

Franz and Frieda share the driving, since Miss Augusta and I do not know how. We are traveling in a 1970 Bonneville pig with tinted electric windows, air conditioning, and a radio with electronically adjustable antenna, which we are supposed to deliver to some guy in Los Angeles. On the shelf below the rear window is a pile of artists' sketch pads (both Miss Augusta and Frieda like to draw) and a stack of pornographic New York papers, which Franz feels are a good present for people with whom we might crash as we cross America, because they are not available everywhere. Franz has made the trip several times before and is not filled with the excitement of the journey, as, in fact, none of us is. Before leaving I tried to read *On the Road* by Jack Kerouac but did not understand long passages where he spreads maps of the continent out on the floor and whispers place names to himself. We spent the first day's drive examining the car for a fool-proof stash, but as always happens, anything that came into our minds we immediately rejected as being the first place the police would look. There was a lot of bickering about this question. Frieda, who was holding a collection of downs which she must have wherever she goes, and also Franz's mescaline, said she might as well hold everything to cut down our vulnerability, but then when she had everything together began to feel she was being sacrificed and became suspicious. Miss Augusta thought the way Frieda was acting was "very interesting" and in her drowsy detached monotone made Frieda feel terrible: insecure, inferior.

April 11. Franz, who spends five or six dollars for cabs every day in New York is on a strange economy-obsessive orgy of frugality. Wants to avoid restaurants for eating and motels for lodging. Wants very much to buy food on the road and prepare it in the car, while on the move. He does not foresee the smell of oranges and salmon and jelly putrefying and clinging to the car. He sees the continent as an obstacle on the path to the Pacific Ocean. Miss Augusta, attempting valiantly to inject herself into the consciousness of others simply through the magnitude, plenitude, and variety of her demands, wants everything changed: the speed of the car, the radio station, tones of voice, diet, the time of daily stopping and starting. Derives greatest pleasure from Franz or me screaming at her rudely. Then her face is a bright star. Whap. In front of you. Glowing and streaming. And unhappy Frieda is asking for ups. Wants me to score speed or diet pills for her. She says she realizes she has been gloomy, now promises smiley face with ups. Give chances when they are so easy to give. Franz beams at her, in love and taking much shit, his mood improving as Frieda grows more and more gloomy, comforting her, kissing her forehead, beaming.

Drove from the highway rest area, where families are crashing in their cars, to St. Louis. Have come to rest in a motel sixty miles west of St. Louis. The car is a rushing mind, will arrive in LA insane. Came into St. Louis at 6 P.M., over the bridges, to an evangelist meeting that was taking place on the broad flat scrub land wide among surrounding highways. The sky timorous black haze and sunset, and there was an orange circus wagon that said, "The Only Peace Is in Christ," with a peace symbol painted on all sides. We arrived just in time to hear, "Jesus Loves Me! Right On! Jesus Loves Me! Right On!" from the crowd of pleasant Midwestern people, well dressed in stadium coats, women wearing little gloves. Saw an old alcoholic kneel under a Bible and be blessed, weeping and grinning, saying, "Oooo, *yes* brother!" Franz snapped pictures of these people, tiny under a spreading purple sunset and all those mid-air highway ramps. An intensely grinning boy with burning orange eyes came over to me, gave the peace fingers, supposedly the sign that made us brothers, him and me, and said, "Howdy, brother, do you have Christ in your heart?" I said I did. He said he was with Arthur Blessitt, the hip evangelist, and they have been touring the nation for two months. He invited me to come to their nightclub on Sunset Strip, called HIS Place, where I could meet people who were seeking salvation. Franz thought all this was unhealthy and kept saying, "Surreal . . . fuckin' surrealistic," but Frieda felt it was nice to see people enjoying themselves, feeling good about their beliefs.

Meeting a believer! What a shock that always is, to perceive that there are people at home in their conceptual universes, optimistic and at home. St. Louis was under this distant black sky. The parks were damp and cool. In clumps of yellow and white, with sashes of blue and red, little children and their families appeared on and around the steps of the Civic Center. A sign above said that Fred Waring and His Pennsylvanians were playing tonight. The people were relaxed, patient and smiling. I was talking to a guy I had just met who said he was an usher in the Civic Center. He was in his car across the street drinking wine. I was telling him about Arthur Blessitt and he was peering at the people, mumbling, his hatred for them growing and growing as he sat there. I said I thought St. Louis was ready for voodoo. This caught his attention and he started asking the families as they went by his car, "You ready for voodoo man?" drinking the wine, smacking his lips, "You ready for voodoo," he was saying, with the bitterest edge to his voice. Then he got out of his car, slammed the door and stomped angrily off to work in his blue usher's uniform, saying as he went, in a voice not too loud but about barroom conversational, "You all ready for this voodoo?"

Motel tonight. Franz has paid for a single room, but he and Frieda and I are all in it. Miss Augusta sleeps outside in the car, with the tape recorder, sleeping under coats because she does not want to split the cost of the room.

Frieda entered the room and broke down crying. Franz now comforting her with reason and compassion. It was not her fault she couldn't drive more than a half hour today. She will do better tomorrow. He is not tired. He is not angry. He does love her. Miss Augusta did not mean what she said. I did not mean what I said. (This I affirmed.) Franz did not mean what he said. He does love her. Just as much. Not even a tiny, tiny bit less. Not a tiny bit. Frieda's mood is improving and she admits her touchiness is due to constipation and not having any ups. She will be better tomorrow. "Shit is an amazing thing," says Franz. He recalls a comic book with a picture of a man squatting on a hillside at sunrise, shitting heftily and smokily, and sighing, "Ah, ah, I'm holy again." In later frames another man is walking by, hands clasped behind his back, who has not moved his bowels, sunrise to sunrise, for four days. He says, "I'm a sinner, I'm a sinner."

Frieda thinks this is a cut at her, and plunges again into the worst of moods.

April 14. The moment when the music of the radio merges with the landscape to become the climax of a movie. Stirring landscape. We think of ourselves poignantly as these four silent Eastern sick people in a rush car to the West Coast, listening to this music that is actually playing, rolling through actual Kansas as we really are, only in a movie. Everything, at these moments, is touching and mellow, as the music on the radio and the landscape respond to each other in the most delicate ways. Now it is raining. Flash of still cows grazing in wet loam. It rains so hard the cows sink, standing in place, into the earth. Their chins lie flat across the mud surface and they are mooing in wonder.

Arriving in Kansas City early afternoon, Franz wanted to see the slaughterhouses. In an area similar to the dock area of other cities we saw a huge ramshackle maze of corridors and ramps stacked and crisscrossing in three layers in the air. Everything was made of old lumber. There were no walls, only widely spaced planks over the corridors hanging in the air, which were the livestock runs, along which pigs and cattle were driven to pens where they were put on auction and then driven off by the buyers. Franz wanted to take pictures, and he and I went up one of the ramps off a huge field of grass and rubble into a cool dark corridor which was wide enough in some places to have rows of corrals in some of which there were pigs still languishing although it was late in the day and the auctioning was done. We heard yelling and a scratchy shuffling sound, and this got louder until we saw a herd of pigs pushing and pressing down one of the ramps to our level. The pigs were packed tight together, either straining to keep their heads high for air or with their heads between the legs of other pigs. They were sneezing and grunting, squealing, slipping, and falling. At the rear of the herd were two young boys who seemed to be having a good time. They were both dressed like cowboys, with cowboy hats, chaps, and spurs. When one of the pigs was not keeping up with the crowd they would have to move it with short whips, and they liked to get on the backs of the pigs, digging their spurs into the pigs' sides to make them shoot ahead and squeal. Franz was taking pictures one after the other, and these guys posed smiling on the backs of some pigs, riding them with their arms flung out. A few minutes after this herd had passed us, going down another ramp to ground level, another sneezing, foaming herd was rushing down the ramp. Two more boys were at the rear of this herd, also dressed like cowboys, barking guttural commands which sounded like they had once been words but had evolved into pig noises. Franz stood on top of one of the fences to photograph the dark turbulent section of the corridor the pigs were passing through. These boys also posed on the backs of pigs, laughing and flailing their arms over the intense, intelligent, and confused faces of the pigs, who were like a panicked crowd. One photograph Franz took, showing the airiness and the levels of confinement of this place, has these pigs pressing down the ramp away from us, while twenty feet above them, moving along another slatted alley at right angles to the pigs, a herd of cows going slowly to slaughter, and showing through between these two crowds, an immense sign across the river with a smiling cow and a smiling pig that says SWIFT standing up in the bright blue sky.

In the second rush of pigs there was one pig, among

the larger ones but not the largest, a dusty white, that was loudly quacking in terror or anger, and throwing itself into strange contortions as it shuffled along with the others. At first this pig, who was near the center, tried to climb over the backs of other pigs. Then it shouldered into them, making its pained quacking noise, until it had cleared a space around itself inside of which, while the herd was in motion, this pig turned itself around and barreled into the pigs behind it, going the other way. When he made it to the rear of the herd one of the boys ran in front of him, shouting his commands and snapping the short whip, but the pig ran through his legs and knocked him down. It ran up the ramp it had just come down, until it reached a barrier, which it butted into over and over again but which it could not move. The two boys tried to force the pig down the ramp. It seemed ultimately inevitable that they would succeed, because the sections of fencing were constructed so that each part of the ramp's walls could be swung on a hinge to turn it into a door. They swung the section that was impeding the pig until it was almost flat with another wall, trapping the pig in a vise, then opening another small section for it to escape through into the passage where they wanted it to go. All this time the pig quacked and shrieked. The two boys rode it, kicked it, whipped it. The pig butted and sideswiped at them and tried to climb the fences. Another herd was coming down the ramp, so the two boys had to leave this pig and catch up with the others. Franz took photographs of the pig making its way, like a man with an urgent message, through this new herd, all the way to the back, where two more boys tried to capture it. The other pigs did not seem curious about this one. They let it pass when they could and did not turn to watch what it was doing.

We watched it struggle through several herds of pigs, never allowing itself to be pushed further down the ramp than the place where we were, but never getting further up the ramp either. Before leaving, we said something about the white pig to one of the boys, who said every now and then there is one like that. He said when the rest of the pigs were all in the slaughterhouse, they would have to come back and take this one alone, section by section of movable fence.

Franz and I went away excited and happy to have seen a hero of the pigs on our first visit to a stock yard. Frieda and Miss Augusta were waiting in the car, smoking and talking, and we told them what we had seen. Miss Augusta wanted to run over there and take some pictures with her Polaroid, for *Life*'s "Face of America" photo contest, but we told her it was all over. The white pig was probably caught and killed by now. The description of pigs and cows going to their deaths, and the courage of this one pig, were very moving to both girls. They tried to think of a solution. Frieda said she would never eat meat again, only vegetables, but I told her that scientists have recorded the screams of tomatoes being sliced and there are graphs of the panic of maple leaves threatened with fire. Miss Augusta ruminated on the problem for a while and then decided what the country needs is a revolution. Franz and I, on the other hand, were for a short time feeling bloodthirsty. We wanted to stay in Kansas City another day to witness the miracle of slaughter, Franz saying, "There are so many *things* in the world. What do you think we're traveling for?" But he drove us out of the city.

April 15. Woke up in Denver. Seven-dollar motel. We do not think about saving money any more. Franz likes to make regular stops at diners and rest areas. Miss Augusta has a terrible time with food. She can only eat the best of foods, and only a few kinds. Constantly, in gritty diners in the middle of Kansas, Miss Augusta, on seeing fried shrimp on the menu, asks the waitress, "These fried shrimp? Are they fresh?" The waitress is flabbergasted. Miss Augusta looks at Franz and me with a superior hate, like an overthrown monarch forced by circumstances to associate with stooges, to remind us of all the times we have not bothered to find a restaurant where she *could* eat the food, and says to the waitress, "I'll just have coffee, thank you." She drinks coffee curled up in the corner of the booth, holding her cup with both hands, rolling her head slightly to allow the steam of the coffee to scald her whole face, and smiling peacefully into the center of the cup. We are afraid. She eats nothing. She has ten cups of coffee each day. She talks incessantly and bitterly, often threatening to tell us, and especially me, things about ourselves that she has been too kind to tell us till now. We, and especially I, do not want to know these things. And she has alternate moments of good-natured friendship which make her hard to hate. We will take her to a Chinese restaurant. We are resolved.

Arrived in Boulder, where there was a student strike at 11,000 feet. Enjoyed talking to students, who were trying to develop a crisis consciousness in the middle of an easy picturesque campus. On or off strike all students and most other residents of Boulder are found in the student cafeteria, where Franz and I circulated among the tables looking for ups, which are always found in student cafeterias.

Spring. The travels are starting. Everyone is beginning to think about moving around, looking for new scenes. A great number of people say they are going to Eugene, Oregon, for some reason. No one who says he is going to Eugene has a reason. I ask what is there, and they say a college. Met a young couple of fourteen from Baltimore. They are going to Eugene. He sells acid when he has the capital, and now in Boulder, acid is free or nearly free, so this kid is picking up all the free acid he can and taking it to Eugene, which I never heard of before this week but which this kid says is a very big thing. It is his theory that there are only two things that motivate the American longhair, as he refers to us, anthropologically, to move, and these things are music and geography. Next year, according to him, everyone will go to Alaska. "You'll see me there," he says, "just spacin' around, sellin' my acid. Be a million longhairs in Alaska next year, and I'll be there too." Miss Augusta takes his picture for the "Face of America" contest, saying, "You're both so beautiful."

Spending the night in some community crash pad in Boulder, a building that seems to have been designed for Bible study, recreation and dances, but which has been donated for perpetual crashing of the massive freak influx expected every summer. We were served a macrobiotic meal, wet and yellow-brown, eaten with the fingers, very good bread and tea. Most of the people here are young, fifteen or sixteen. Everyone has the serious face of someone preoccupied with the multiple details of a long journey, and most are well provisioned. Huge, lightweight backpacks with some clothes, musical instruments, paperbacks, and everyone has a little toiletries kit with which he stands in line at the sinks. Tonight, as acid is free in Boulder, not too many people will go to sleep. Franz is taking pictures of the stars of the place, two older men named Brother Robert and Shawn, both having biker clothes with flags sewn onto the jackets. They are posing in typical goon manner: hats askew, tongue stuck out one side of the mouth, eyes crossed. Brother Robert is in charge of this place and tells me he is the one who convinced the minister and congregation to donate the building. He goes to the phone in an office full of Bibles and old magazines, makes calls in search of a place to crash. He says he has to get away from all these crashers. The office is full of kids tripping. Someone is freaking out and is balled up, clenched, on a couch, saying, "Who did I hurt? Who did I *hurt?*" with his eyes shut tight. Others are sitting around him, gazing at him, smoking ciga- rettes. They are prepared in case he tries to do anything rash. I offer some of the downs which Frieda always has, but the others refuse for the one who is freaked out, saying that whenever one uses downs to avoid a rough trip, one is always sorry the next day for wasting good acid. As it gets later, the whole place assumes the air of an emergency ward. It is very late now, and the halls and stairs are packed with people smoking and talking urgently. Everyone seems to be waiting for election returns. Miss Augusta went to sleep upset, because when she tried to use the ladies' room, she was thrown out by a girl who was sleeping there. "Who turned that light on?" Miss Augusta heard when she got to the bathroom. "Get out of here or I'll kill you! And I'm not kidding!" said the girl. Miss Augusta turned out the light and used the men's room. It is not easy to sleep here, on the floor of the ping-pong room. Out in the hall, Brother Robert is entertaining the kids. "Y'ever ball on grass, man? Y'ever ball on grass or hash? That's the best way. One time I was so spaced out, man, I thought I was a printing press.

Fuckin' printing press. My wife asks me what I'm doin', I say, 'Shut up I got two thousand more copies to go.' "

The next day we are woken up at seven. Group effort to clean the place and move the ping-pong tables to their original positions on the floor. Everyone must be out by eight-thirty. We are allowed to hang around outside, though, on green sunny lawns. I went back to get something at ten and the place was transformed. There was a receptionist at the door, the halls were clean and smelled of pine-scented deodorant, and in the office with the phone, the minister was greeting a man with a briefcase.

On the peak, 15,000 feet, the Great Divide, walking around in the snow, which is still at the tops of the mountains. Amazing to see seven cities to the east, a wide plain with some parts under clouds and dark, others in the sunlight, so wide we could see the slope of the globe. The wind almost blows you off the mountain. All wind and lungs.

April 16. We had a strange ride, losing ourselves in forests and on the ledges of mesas, nonchalant and stoned, in search of this place Libre. Libre has a reputation for elegant geodesic domes, and we feel we should see it before we go to New Mexico. Driving and stopping, forgetting where we were, we were surprised to see the sun going down and blackness all around us before we had gotten to Libre. When we did get there we were nervous and tired. Got out of the car and walked over a stream to the first dome. All the domes, as far as we could see, were solid and colorful, and looked as though they belonged in the center of a living room in an apartment in New York. Some of the domes were surrounded by works of art. There were large colorful shapes which were very ugly, like giant crumpled objects. Painting easels stood on the hillsides, facing the sunset. As we entered the clearing in which these domes were standing, a woman who seemed to be working at her sink saw us through her hexagonal window. She squinted at us. We smiled at her. Miss Augusta flashed the peace sign, probably assuming that this woman was at that moment sharing with us the relief of having arrived safely and seeing her there in her kitchen. The woman looked at us for a moment, as if trying to place us, then, wiping her hands on the front of her long dress, called to someone to her left. A man's head appeared at another hexagonal window to the left of the woman. Profile of this man's head, shouting something to the woman. Profile of the woman, exasperated, shouting something back. Both faces disappear, too fast to know in which direction, then the door of the dome opens outward toward us and the woman appears. She is upset and annoyed that we are hard to see in the dark. "Who are you?" she says. Behind her we can see the man, seated on the floor, eating food from a bowl he is holding a few inches from his face, eating very fast, handful after handful, not looking toward the door. We do not know what to answer to the question of who we are. "Hi," says Franz. "What do you want?" asks the woman. We said we were looking for a place to crash. "Well, who *are* you?" asks the woman again. And then, after a while, as if in explanation, she says, "We've changed our policy. I'm sorry," and closes the door.

Unfriendliness, unkindness, on the part of hippies

(freaks, longhairs, whatever) toward other hippies is not as uncommon as one would imagine it to be. Generally, except in areas where there are few hippies or where there is a sense of crisis, as in riots, or where a crowd of hippies has just seen a movie about hippies, we do not go out of our ways for one another. Hitch-hiking, even in San Francisco, teaches that businessmen, salesmen, college professors, and lonely veterans with new moustaches are more likely to give you a ride than a longhair. Longhairs tend to be embarrassed among people who possess less than they do. While most people like to share their dope, they feel uncomfortable sharing their food or clothing, albums or camera equipment. This has to do with conspicuous consumption, a concept I little understand but which I take to mean in this case: people can tell you have a lot of clothes if they see you around wearing a lot of clothes, they can tell you have an expensive car if they see you in your car, but the only way for them to know you have a lot of dope is for you to give it to them.

Of course, almost all people, straight or hip, place great value on the things they own, but it is sometimes discouraging to see particular moments of ungenerosity among hippies and to perceive that, all publicity for the evolved consciousness or a tribal closeness among us notwithstanding, our human affinities are often determined by our wealth. Hippies in their homes do not like crashers, hippies at dinner do not like visitors, hippies on their way to the beach do not like riders. This seems to be because many people who are hip suspect that other people are using a disguise of hipness to rip them off. Most communes exclude free-loaders and have elaborate twisted rules about use of the telephone and refrigerator.

Older hippies, and hippies firmly entrenched in some set of beliefs (either mystical or political), are usually the stingiest and have good reasons for holding on to what they have that are in perfect accord with their faith. When I was in Berkeley, right after the National Guard shot four students at Kent State in Ohio and all the schools in the country were on strike, and the stock market was dropping every day, and all over Berkeley breathless leftists were waiting for a crash, someone stood up at a meeting of the Berkeley Strike Committee, 10,000 assembled students in the gym, and suggested that students all over the country immediately sell whatever stocks they have and in that way topple the market. For a while it seemed this would be a popular resolution, but someone else pointed out that this was a bad time to sell and everyone was sure to lose money, so the matter was dropped. At Libre, they did not like to have visitors because they had always had a lot of visitors and this disturbed the flow and grace of their lives there. In traveling I have found that it is best to meet people who do not have things, are young, and live in places that have been torn apart or are temporary, because these people are generally kinder to strangers, hip or not.

We did not try any of the other domes. We got back in the car and left. Spent the night down the road with some Meher Baba enthusiasts from Harvard. These people cooked very well and Miss Augusta had a lot to eat. Pleasant night discussing injustice, which seems to comprise the great majority of conversation in every place. We shared anecdotes of injustice to the American Indian and the Japanese-American during the Second World War. When I tried to draw the discussion toward injustice to the labor unions, which I had just read some books about, these people were not interested, but they knew a lot about injustice to the farmers, especially during the Depression of 1929.

Early afternoon. Car pulled in to mud forms and mud terrace of wet day. Community of smashed, leaking domes built years ago by the people who are now at Libre but abandoned by those people and left for nomads to inhabit. Everything in disrepair, grimy. The present occupants feel no sense of possessiveness in regard to the structures on the property. They do not care what happens to the structures although in rain they are grateful for whatever coherence there is in the seams of the domes. As soon as the car stopped a boy opened the screen door of the largest dome and asked us if we had any dope. We said we did. He invited us in. There were ten or twelve kids standing around a stove on the lower level of a huge split-level floor, frying potatoes and onions in a black pan, rolling cigarettes from a giant yellow can of Top tobacco, emptying potfuls of rain into the sink and putting these pots back under the leaks in the roofline. Everyone seemed to have a cold. Franz and I rolled joints and soon everyone was mellow and hilarious, and they told us what it is like to live there in the winter. Said going into town for food stamps and then buying food was their only activity. Late in the winter, dope became very scarce and, though there is a small pipe-making industry at Drop City, they usually had nothing to smoke. Most of the people were very young, said they were runaways from distant states, told incredible stories about their parents in which the most incredible detail is the massive number of parents who place their kids in mental institutions. There was much reminiscence about mental institutions, which most of the people found to be the best place for meeting people, especially beautiful chicks who had been committed for nymphomania and for scoring acid.

Franz was asked to drive some people into town so they could get their food stamps, and someone wanted to bring his dog to a vet. Somehow hearing that a car was leaving for town, a crowd gradually filtered into the largest dome from the other domes, people who needed things in the town. They said there are fewer than a car a day at this time of the year passing through Drop City.

The name Drop City: one guy said this is because the domes look like bird droppings on the plain; another said when the original owners of the place were building their houses, a motorcycle gang named the Droppers, because they liked to drop things on their enemies, had helped out, and the name was in honor of their friendship. A chick named Jan said the name signified that it was OK to drop in at any time. She said she came here three months ago and has not been off the land since then. She had a message for me to deliver. For some reason she had never written a letter. *From Jan Scott Telepathic Receiver: Maria is dead after private plane crash south of German Border 15th September 1969.* She made me promise to deliver this information to a certain address in Chicago. She said, "These people are awful worried, awful awful worried, I have to tell them what I know, I don't have the money for a stamp."

It rained all afternoon. After the potatoes and onions were done, the pan was passed around for us to take what we wanted. Immediately someone started cooking something else, a pot of brown rice, and when this was done and eaten, something else was cooked. In this way, most of the residents of Drop City spent the afternoon gathered around the stove, eating and smoking, waiting for the car to return with food. Some people had a stack of questionnaires from the Department of Sociology at Fordham University which they could not decide whether to destroy or fill out and send in. The questionnaire, after going into the family background, education and religion of the communards complying, lists thirty-three "values" and asks if living on a commune realizes these values. 1. close interpersonal relationships, 2. chance to be alone sometimes, 3. total honesty with other people, 4. doing things with other people, 5. a sense of community, 6. keeping yourself together, 7. being content without luxuries, 8. being satisfied with the necessities of life, 9. personal freedom, 10. personal growth, etc. The questionnaire was discussed. No one could decide if Drop City was living up to any of this. Some of the values (23. a sensuous life, 26. living a truly Christian life, 29. personal growth through drug use) were so far from anyone's actual daily life there—remember scarcity of dope— that the questionnaire made some people depressed and initiated a discussion of plans for futures when things would be better, when they would be doing things that had some value.

When Franz came back he said, "I'm not upset, not at all, but I feel I've been taken advantage of. I understand. I mean, I understand." He said the people he drove into town had gone to more places in town than they had initially said they were going to, and had been very slow about everything they did. Also, they borrowed money, did not help pay for the gas and somehow they got Franz to buy them each an ice-cream cone. The guy with the dog, a middle-aged man with a beautiful long red beard and small soapy white eyes, came in shouting, "The Age of Aquarius, people! Evolution of human consciousness! My god! The Age of Aquarius!" He was referring to Franz's generosity. "What did I say, people? *Spirits* are coming through Drop City. *Love* is driving through, people!" This was his way of thanking Franz. This man was called The Physicist. He took us to his dome. Aside from the bed and woman he had there, the place looked like the cockpit of a space ship, level upon level of sheet metal, thousands of off-on switches with printed labels below them: "Shiva," "Center of Earth," "Ionosphere modulation," and so on. He wanted to explain what he was doing with all this equipment, but we did not understand. He grew more and more excited as he ran around his apparatus, running up a crude ladder made of logs to show us the features on the second floor. Screaming, "Earthminds, I'm so *bored* with you! How can I *tell* you!" Whenever he screamed his little dog barked and his tail wagged happily. And his woman brought everyone tea. And he grew furious, then resigned, then pleased, then miserable, then furious, but he never touched the switches or turned even one from off to on. This, he said, would be inadvisable to do until there were 144,000 Most Holy Men on the planet, at which time the power of the machine could be controlled.

Taos – The Family

In Taos, New Mexico, we were looking for a place to stay. For a while we slept in a photography gallery in Guadalupe Plaza, a single room partitioned to separate off a small living space in the back. This space, the front area, and all of New Mexico are covered in flesh-colored silt and when you sit down in this State, or lie down to rest, puffs of smoke like exhausted flocks fly out at your sides and resettle over you.

Arrival was at dusk, and pale equivalence of texture and tone was spread over Taos, which we came at downward from a pass through rough mountains beneath whose seasonal rockslide and floods we had driven this gross, bruised Bonneville to beat night. We were afraid to arrive after dark because there are shootings and a frequency of atrocities in the area.

Dusk in Taos in the Spring: nubby gray deepening to a terrified black as strollers and loungers fade from the streets, as the cars come out for trouble or patrol, churning the stones on all the dirty roads of town. We parked the car, and Franz swept the back clear of the maps, cameras, and straw hats that were there, because these, as he said, are an open invitation to get ripped off. We buried this crap on the floor of the car, beneath things least likely to act as a come on, giving the impression of casual filth to hide wealth. I did not understand this maneuver, since the car itself, great pig, looked ripe for demolition as it was, alone in the great, chained Plaza, nose toward the only line of hippie business establishments in Taos. These businesses, The Tihuana Taco, a pizza place and café; The One Loose Eye, where we were to stay; a clothing store and a

sandalmaker, were the prime in-town targets for ter-
rorists, and all but The One Loose Eye had bullet holes
in their windows.

Before going in to sleep, we went to The Tihuana
Taco for dinner. Miss Augusta, gaunter and gaunter
from a fast that had spanned the continent, could also
not eat pizza, the specialty of the Tihuana Taco. The
rest of us were very hungry. Franz knew the owner
of the place, and said it was the only restaurant in town
that serves hippies. We did not respond to her sug-
gestion that we find another place to eat. Her eyes
made their water of extremest frustration which gave
them a shine. She said she was going out by herself
to find food. Everyone in the Tihuana Taco took note.
Miss Augusta was strongly urged to stay put, but she
went into the night. Later she was back, red as
blood and viciously scandalized. Some Chicano boys
had chased her down one of the calm boring streets,
screaming and throwing rocks.

Taos is the second poorest or poorest county in
America. The land is shitty and there is not enough
water to make farming a pleasure or a profit. The
largest source of income for the county has always
been tourism. The tourists are attracted, for some
reason, by the Kit Carson Museum (former dream
house of Kit and his child bride); by the Indian Reservation, where the rain dance is done; by the thirty-five
art galleries in town (a huge number of art galleries
for a place with an impoverished population of 3,000);
and by the D.H. Lawrence Ranch, where many of
Lawrence's paintings can be seen. During the past
three or four years, the population has doubled, and
the new ones are all hippies, come home from their
various exiles, variously in the cities and suburbs in
America, home to the Land.

In their coming, they have made many enemies among the people who were there, wherever, before them. I can remember long before I actually got to New Mexico hearing strange horror stories about the place. One, which is widely told and believed on the East Coast, but which fewer and fewer have heard of, have knowledge of, the farther West you travel, is about the Motherfuckers, the New York chapter of SDS. The Motherfuckers, feeling the heat too heavily in New York, decided to break camp and roam nomadic across the country. In northern New Mexico, they settled down for a while, presumably to seclude themselves and train for guerrilla combat. After a short time in their new home, one of the Motherfuckers stole something—sometimes you hear pig and sometimes you hear goat—from a tribe of local Indians. The Indians caught him and then with the consent of the guerrillas, made him a slave. He is now, according to this story, serving a sentence of eight years, working sunrise to sunset for the Indians. I do not think this is true, but many people in New York are in its thrall and bring it up whenever someone mentions going to the country. Other stories, which are true, include scalpings, beatings and rapes perpetrated upon hippies by Chicanos and beatings, rapes and shootings perpetrated by the hippies upon the Chicanos (or whatever the indigenous population of the popular area happens to be).

The Chicanos in Taos are working-class poor, in general, and they deeply resent the money and leisure of the hippies. They also believe the hippies to be immoral and atheistic. They are afraid the dissolute quality of the freaks' life styles will corrupt their children, who are having a tough enough time as it is without grooming themselves to be further unemployable. However, the antipathies of the Catholic lower class may not be the full explanation for the trouble in Taos. There is a seasonal nature to the violence, which swells every spring and subsides as the summer tourist season begins, and it is suspected the Taos business community begins its establishment, in some way controls the flow of aggression against the hippies. Whether or not this is true, I know there are a lot of Chicanos in Taos who are unbelievably, almost comically, disgusted by longhairs. While I was there pickup trucks would often stop and beefy men would call out, "Get a haircut, you dirty hippie," in imitation of the slogans that rang out and were done with ringing in other neighborhoods around the nation years ago. The first night we were in Taos we used only candlelight and crept over the floor of the gallery keeping our heads below the windows, hardly speaking, hearing no music, to hide the fact that The One Loose Eye was occupied. The next morning the tires of the standard prehistoric Oldsmobile had been slashed, and it sat down flat in the dirt.

At this time I was running out of money and I was tired of traveling. I wanted to settle in Taos for a while and do some work. After visiting two other groups of people, we went to see a group called the Family, in an adobe house about five miles outside of Taos, and I decided to stay there. Franz, Frieda, and Miss Augusta, who met the Family when I did, were also drawn to these people, who were smiling, hugging, decomposing from intensity to intensity like children, but they didn't feel they could stay there. Franz and Frieda, after bringing me my suitcase from town, went on to Los Angeles to deliver the car. Franz took pictures before he left, and Frieda played with the babies and animals that were in general circulation around the property. On their way to LA, they stopped in Reno, where Franz lost all their money and where they were married. As for Miss Augusta, she stayed in Taos, in a motel, to get some drawing done. I didn't see her while she was in town and I was with the Family, except once in passing from the Family truck. She was thinner than ever, with a round straw hat to keep her face in shade, drawing the portrait of the old Indian who was wearing a blanket and a baseball cap. One night she was sitting with some guy in his car when a group of Chicanos walked over, opened the doors and dragged them both out into the street. They beat up the guy she was with but didn't hurt Miss Augusta, and people I know who saw her after that said she had grown gaunt and talked incessantly, insanely, to everyone she met. She was fed up, she said. In a short time she got a ride out of Taos, I think to California, where she had some friends.

At the Family, they had discovered the meaning of life, and when I first saw them I was stunned by the presence, in the faces and voices, of idealistic beliefs. During my life I have not had the opportunity to observe people fervent in their beliefs to the point of evangelicism. Arthur Blessitt ("Jesus turns me on") the hip preacher from LA was the first man I'd spoken with who had, in the flesh, those eyes and that resonance that are the thrown-open doors leading to a man's fanaticism.

The Family was transcendent: completely improbable: not deducible at first attempt from the data of America at this time. All in and around this house, like contented dukes and dowagers, faces afloat in a joy and good will that were prefainting lush and dawn rose, the sixty some odd husbands and wives did their daily jobs. The day I was first there and first met the Family, birds were being hysterectomized for Passover in the kitchen and pansful of liver, like purplish fish in small pools of blood, were being dealt into the oven, one by one, for chopped liver. I said, "What do I have to do to stay here?" A man with a sensitive sad upper face and a sensitive happy lower face said, "Nothing." He paused at the abyss of simplicity and then did not jump in. Everyone in the kitchen was silent, hands that were plunged in cavities of chicken did not budge or scoop. I was aware that there was some importance in this moment: a stranger comes to the Family, and consequently this man who had taken it upon himself to answer my question had placed himself in a position of responsibility. "And everything," he said, thus schematizing the labyrinth of paradox into which every question or objection to the Family goes, and out of which nothing comes but harmony: hypnotic smile. I said, "What do you mean?" He said, "You'll find out." Conspiratorial glances. Everyone smiled at me with the tenderness and concern all people who place themselves in the position of the initiate must receive, in all groupings that are grouped around what they feel to be knowledge.

We did not want to say any more and he left. For a while I passed the time in the kitchen, asking names, helping with the pronunciation of my own, and explaining myself to the people, who were all friendly. They were making preparations for a feast, a Passover Seder. Most of the Family are not Jewish.

The Family is an extended marriage. This means that everyone is married to everyone else. The first night I was there, Lord George, who is a dropout from rabbinical school and a previous resident of Shaker Heights in Cleveland, stopped on his way from the bathroom to the bus, where he slept, and asked me if I knew "how sleeping works around here." I did not. He told me there are not enough beds to go around.

Sixty people live in three rooms, and at night all available floor space is covered with mattresses. Members of short standing usually sleep on these mattresses, while the more permanent residents sleep on huge carpentered double-decker beds, sometimes three to a bed. The beds belong to the women. If you want to sleep in a bed, or if you want to sleep with a woman, you are supposed to ask her at some time during the day if it is all right with her. Lord George said, "Now, she'll want to know if you want to fuck her or if you just want to sleep with her. If she's already been asked, and she's got a man for the night, she might tell you to come by a little after bedtime and you can share the bed with them." I asked if there were any chicks it was for some reason not cool to ask, although throughout the day I had not noticed any incidents of particularized affection between people, only an equivalent warmth and affection among everyone and directed toward everyone. For the most part contact among these people was without sexual overtone, and when sexuality was implied, as with Lady Maya, a moonfaced, olive faced, olive-eyed girl who hugged and growled when men came near her, it was a general implication, a habit of affection. Lord George said it was cool to ask anyone. Some people, he said, were doing a thing, but it was still cool to ask.

At bedtime, after all the asking has been done and arrangements have been made for the night, everyone sits around on their beds and mattresses playing nude War or Fish, treating themselves to the several natural releases and relaxations of the body, the burps, farts, scratches, and clinical self-examinations of the end of the day, picking through their faces and the folds of their skins for impurity. Reading each other letters from home, the documentation that the perverted past

[118]

is still alive around them, dark with concepts like, "I am enclosing some money. Please don't let anyone know you have it, as it is for you and the baby." Discussing people who have left the family and the fates that befell them: busted, busted, insane, busted, married, stranded in the East, a junkie busted; and touching the ones they are in bed with, preparing for love. Opening night for me was spent in a sleeping bag below the kitchen table, with my head tuned in to the crackle of the Family radio communications central control receiver, which was in the pantry. Soon after the lights went out in all the rooms a voice that had come here from Brooklyn was raised in a whining protest. It was a pregnant girl in the next room complaining about one of her breasts. "My boo-ub! Ooh it hu-urts." Another girl asked what was the matter with it. A masculine voice grumbled. The girl from Brooklyn said there was a hard lump under the nipple. The light was flicked on and couples caught in midfuck froze, while Lady Heather examined the breast and advised that this girl squirt some milk out for relief.

Every night when the lights went out there would be a ten-minute tremor of passion in the rooms, then silence until morning. Everything will be denied. The past is lost to the dramatic past, which is the real use of experience.

These raggy memories of the Family: coughs; a chain of harsh instances. Remembered at this distance sharp hacks of texture into the full sandy blank. I am a careless reporter; I took no notes, except on the subject of myself, and these turn out to be a record of unreasonable poses, various attitudes and angles of reaction to the firm unembraceable pose of the Family itself, which for a long time in my mind has not had the precarious quality of a recognizably real thing but has been either a caricature or evaporated, gone. I believe that lies leave a clearer impression than the truth. The past is lost to the dramatic present. The way one talks to oneself, within one's own mind, leaves almost no impression at all. Recently I realized that I always talk to myself in slang. I address myself as man; I ask myself, what's happening, man; I wake up in the mornings and the pose is so certain I say the day is out of sight. After so many years of carelessness in consulting myself, I have no faith that what I tell myself is coming from any essential inner me. The notes I have on the Family reflect both my own comic posturing ("I will stay here for the rest of my life!") and theirs (Lord Sean said to me today, "Elia, we're like a fraternity, only we want to pledge the whole *world*."), but there are no true pictures.

The following, written two months after the non-fact, was first splattered all over the floor of a tent at Wheeler's Ranch in California in little notes of past captured under camper cookware.

Everything will be denied. Writing about the Family so shortly after leaving them, and what comes readily before the mind's eye, balloonlike, inhumanly glowing, the verbal slogans and facial slogans of intelligent people forging a path into superstition and ignorance they hope the whole world will use. There are phrases that fall from the blank sky onto otherwise smoothly rolling trains of thought. "We are the losers who decided to become winners." The way, in despair of ever understanding or affecting the geographical world, we are all beginning to retreat into the spirit, feeding it and overloving it with obsessively balanced diets and attentive compilations of those two dictatorial invisibilities, bad and good karma, carving out for ourselves national parks in the mind, away from the world and wooded with welfare and money from home. "I'm god, You're god. We're all god." And as a group, and each inside himself, the Family are perverse cohabitations of fiercely functional and mystical beings whose spiritual preoccupation is a distant world of better men and women, all alive in vast extended families like hives and all aligned in harmony through some as yet undiscovered union of several Oriental religions (or parts of religion), *The Aquarian Gospel of Jesus the Christ* (a vision that came to an American minister named Levi just before the Civil War), *Stranger in a Strange Land* by Robert Heinlein, and the gestalt therapy techniques of Frederick (known around the Family as Fritz) Perls. They go about the daily jobs of the current unregenerate days without ever losing sight of the larger process, ongoing and ongoing while the dishes are washed and business done, of the spiritual evolution of mankind. And this was the most interesting part of it, that like missionaries they themselves are leading exemplary lives in the name of something which in itself has done primarily harm to the world: religion.

The Family in fact is self-consciously guiding itself through the early stages of a new religion. Every day new rituals and customs are tried, and daily the conversation of one person to another is to a greater degree a litany of standard phrases which, like the phrases that become standard in politics, advertising or any other religion, tend to blot out the real world piece by piece until everything in each day is completely comprehensible within the framework of the Family and nothing is real.

Right away I was in love with the Family, and I wanted to stay there, because everything was at first as distant and strange as if I had traveled down the Amazon, and I was astounded that there were actually people of my own age in my own country who were completely unrecognizable to me, whose motives for action I could not understand. But after a while the place began to seem as though it were an intentional reservation formed by its several college graduates into a model anthropological site taken from books about the Indian tribes and Africa.

I didn't like the way they looked there. Their hair is short; they are clean; there are no beards. They say they have cut it loose, like all their clothes and all their things they had when they came here. The idea is to find out what it is about yourself you prize, what it is you have been assuming defines you, and then to get rid of it. I said I was a writer and was threatened with the destruction of my notebooks. Man alone, anti-fabulous, without accouterments, the spirit shining through a trimmed wick. I didn't like the way they looked, and though I knew they were right in every way I tried to keep my hair. I did this by making flamboyant declarations of impatience for a haircut so they would look for other things to take away from me first.

The first possession to go was my name. Everyone's name is changed. Some people get other people's names. It is no small loss, the loss of a lifelong signal, one's own little bell. My name was changed to Mark, which is a name I have never noticed in the world in particular, and I forgot it was my name almost as soon as it was given to me. In the time I was there I never managed to answer to the name Mark. Often, someone starting out to make a casual request of me would be blue in the face before I answered. They said, at first, it was OK, because they all had been that way in the beginning. However, after a while my inability to learn my name annoyed everyone. Once I was reading a book, in the corner of a crowded room and was forced to stop because the noise in the room had reached an unbelievable crescendo. Fifteen people were chanting "Mark! Mark! Mark! Mark!" dancing around, slamming the walls with their palms. I didn't know how long this had been going on; as soon as they had my attention they all stopped and a girl said she wanted to borrow a pencil.

Lord Byron, who is in every way the leader, the warlord, the chief religious adviser of the group, refers to himself as its treasurer and treasure. After my arrival at the Family, I found I was the only one there with ready cash and was buying cigars and cigarettes for a lot of people; also I was sneaking out to buy large breakfasts in a local luncheonette, because health food makes me sick ("That's all the shit that's in you from all the shit food you been eating," I have been told, but whenever I try to make the switch over to purity I am nauseous, gaseous and dizzy for so long I have to give up) and I was not eating with the Family. Lord Byron introduced himself to me and said I was to give him all my money for the treasury. I did so, without hesitation. I gave him ten dollars. There was a much larger sum in traveler's checks that daily I was tempted to turn over to him, but they were somewhere else in Taos with some other things of mine, and even at the times of my greatest passion for the Family, even in the group sings and multiple embraces, I was holding on to my getaway money.

Passover. The Family lives in a tiny adobe house, on no land, outside of Taos. There is no room in it large enough for them all to eat together, so most meals are served out of big pots in the kitchen and carried around the house, eaten crosslegged on the floor, or outside the house, or in one of the cars and buses that is around. They rent another house, though, in town, where half the people work during the day (teaching school, editing a magazine, plotting the publicity for their tedious lovable movie about Taos) and every time there is any excuse—Thanksgiving, Christmas, birth or victory in Reno—the Family transports the stay-at-home half up to this other house, where there is a big living room, and they can all eat together. Now it's Passover and that is as good as any occasion.

Lord George will preside. Lord George is the one from Shaker Heights in Cleveland, and he studied to be a rabbi for two years. He is also a filmmaker. He is the one who finagled the backing for the Family's film, and the co-operation (passivity) of the generally anti-media community of communes around Taos. He has the sharp strange face of an intelligent old man who finds everything amusing except himself, which he finds dynamic and thrilling. I have just read about the Family in *Rolling Stone,* one of those articles with little pictorial dollops between the informational paragraphs to make you feel you are really there. In this article, Lord George is called Lord Ben David (was that his name?) and I learned that he is "twenty-eight, clean-shaven, suave, handsome, mysterious," which stature he almost did attain on Passover, when he wore a skullcap and a prayer shawl and explained the symbolism behind the things on our plates. "This [apples and honey] is the mortar from which the people of Israel made bricks in the years of their bondage. . . . This is the lamb shank which the people of Israel used to smear lamb's blood on their doors so the angel of Death would recognize their homes and pass over them. . . ." We were sitting on the floor around an arc of low tables covered with red and blue cloths. The food was very fine. The children sat at a dais in the center of the room, squealing and destroying. Nathan was supposed to read the blessing over the meal. He said this is my body. This is my blood. Matzoh and Manischewitz. The lights were out and all our faces were shadows and red, crying.

In the Passover service what comes next is the story of the Jews' escape to Israel. Instead, Lord George asked those who knew it to tell the story of the Family. This was part of the conscious evolution of a tribal ritual. Everything was done carefully, in every testimony was the labor of carrying something full and not letting anything spill. In recollections, an exodus from Berkeley, California, to Mesa, Arizona, in a bus was told, and they talked about the ranch-style house they lived in there, and some hassles, words like "hassles" moved off to the distance with the resonance of biblical prose, and then their coming to Taos, New Mexico, "a dying town, without any love" and reviving it by serving it. Spontaneously, possessed by precious memories, people stood and spoke one by one around the room. "The Family started beneath a bridge in Berkeley, where one man knew the truth, and spoke the truth, and another man heard the truth and understood the truth."

"And what was the truth, Lord Byron?"

"The truth was that god is a man: he is a man serving a man, and so he is a god serving a man, and a god serving a god. He is men serving men. The truth is we are all god. We love each other in our godhood; we are royal and holy, and we love all holy men, we love all men. We love god. Gods loving gods. That's the truth."

"What was the truth, Lord Byron?"

"The truth was that I was in despair. I was not even a man. . . ."

[125   ]

"I was too, brother."

"I was, too. But now I love you, and I love myself."

"I was not even a man, I was alone." All around, suddenly shocked by the word "alone," as though remembering painful aloneness and to ward it off, there people are weeping, holding one another, walking after nightmares in each other's arms.

One man stood and said, "I was nothing before I came to the Family, I am nothing without the Family. I am nothing but the Family." Then he almost looked embarrassed, shy to be standing and seen, for a moment, but others were standing too, saying, "I was nothing before I came to the Family. I am nothing without the Family. I am nothing but the Family," and this first man is happy to have thought of something so agreeable to his family. I have never talked to him. He drives the Family bus and has never seemed to be one of the important ones here. Now four people are huddled under his arms and others are around him kissing and saying they love him. He is a happy, drowning man.

How they were so thrilled when I said I was writing a book. "Well," said Lady Maya, "you'll have a lot to say about us. We're incredible." However, at that time, believing I had come to a different era of the world there, writing anything seemed to me a useless drag, and soon I was the man who goes out in the morning after telling his wife he is going to look for a job, then sits in the park reading wet newspapers and eating the lunch she packed. I would sit on a table in the middle of bustling plan-makers, rapturous, catatonic, feeling myself fade and reform, fade and reform behind my face and be asked how my book was coming. I said, fine, fine, but all I had done was to make strange notations of the idiosyncratic and the vague:

"Just had a frightening flash in which the contours of

my mouth did not seem to be in the same room or on the same body as the sounds I spoke. I was immediately silent. In my mind an after-image of lips strangely shaped and placed made me foreign to myself. I feel as though I am changing, part by part. The parts already changed are contemptuous of the unchanged parts. I am not protective of myself. I cannot remember what it was I looked like the last time I saw myself. I was not confident when I spoke the words that were so disembodied. Less and less confident. This confidence, which I used to have, was probably a matter of memory —I had every reason to believe that I would behave as I behaved in my memory's behavior."

Useless. But the Family was very interested in records, evidences of its being. Their movie, which they have sent around the country with cadres of Family exhibitors whom they supply with portable screens and sound systems and each its own publicity kit (posters, handbills, press releases) so it can sweep in spheres of influence from campus to campus, and which the Family takes care of from a room called Central Control, an office like the war room, where a gigantic map of the USA has red pins, black pins, and orange pins (definite, tentative, and present location of teams A, B, C, D, and E) and where the publicity comes out with that hip, grossly sophisticated snideness you see all the time in record ads. . . . "Taos is what is happening in 1970," all that crap, their movie is where most of their money is sunk, so that gets the biggest push right now. After the Family saw this movie, which was edited by some of the Lords, who took it off to Los Angeles to do it like the pros, and the movie was such a wet towel, aimless and wandering from pointless to pointless so that even though they were *in* it they were yawning, the general consensus was that the movie had served its purpose since the Lords that edited it had become closer friends in the process. They said, "We learned a lot from doing it. That's what we *made* the thing for; that's why we do everything. For what we can learn from it, about ourselves and each other." And Lord Byron said that was fine, but now they should see what there was to learn by making back all that money. So they are pushing this film like mad. The art department, the publicity department, Central Control. Graphs are going up on all the walls. Letters are going out to distributors and international festivals, signed, so as not to put the straight world up tight, George Lord or Philip Lord or Mrs. Samantha Lord. Pep talks after dinner. "The team working on the film says we can all start getting ready to go to Japan in the summer. Things are rolling along just fine. We expect an invitation to Expo any minute."

And the message of this movie, the reason it was essential to do it, is to tell people not to come to Taos. All in all, a more serious effort to be uninteresting to the general public has probably never been undertaken in this country; the Family has opened the naturalness of its daily home life so far for several magazines, some newspapers, and a special on ABC. When I was there they were trying to get invited to the Johnny Carson Show, the Merv Griffin Show, the Dick Cavett Show, and the Mike Douglas Show. Letters were going out with that bone-weary "Taos is what's happening in 1970," as an opening line. Lord Sean says we have something to learn from all of these things. He says, "How do I know how I'll react on television? I want to find that out. Why shouldn't I find out everything about myself? Maybe I'll go to the moon someday. How do I know? It's all in life. The Johnny Carson Show is in life. I'm not going to run away from life. I can tell you that."

Lord Sean is also editing the Family magazine, soon to appear, called *Eupsychia*. He wants it to be like *Psychology Today*. "Do you realize, Elia, that *Psychology Today* is the most successful new magazine in America? It has a circulation over 100,000 and advertising on over half the pages. You learn a fuck of a lot more from a successful magazine than a failure." Lord Sean is a dropout (after receiving a Master's) psychology student. He is a very pleasant dogmatic man who, like Lord George, is held together by two things which might tear lesser men apart: a sincere religious fanaticism and an awe-inspiring ambition to be rich. He is scared of "failure." Always talks about it. And no matter what arguments, most of which he will go along with, are used to convince him otherwise, failure is equated in his head with things that do not make money and things that do not, as he puts it, "reach millions and millions and millions of people." When I was there, I was the querulous voice of the hippie. Lord Sean has a winsome anachronistic way of smiling like a Congressman and referring to anyone less militantly motivated away from failure than the Family as "hippie dippies" and to their efforts as "hippie dippy bullshit." He is afraid he will be sucked into the netherworld of hippie dippy bullshit if his magazine is not on the same kind of paper as *Psychology Today*. He is a great theoretician of its avoidance. Once in anger, the querulous voice of the hippies, I accused him of wanting to be rich and famous. He said, "That's what I want to be! Sure it is! There's a whole gestalt to being rich that I feel I should know about."

I woke and the mountains were vague television blue, like remembered mountains. Two white dogs followed me walking up a steep road which was burnt brown and a thread among yellow rectangles of earthstalk. Other dogs barked and faced me down behind fences. From a distance vehicles on a highway are silent tabs, stressless in the distance. When I reached the highway the vehicles were loudly groaning and all the parts of them made great pressured noises against other parts. In vistas and clusters, then, the mountains fields and roads rotated and replaced, as I was walking. Some parts replaced were very strange while other parts were slow and familiar in their motion to the eye that changes position. One bird, another bird. They had heart-red fronts and standing bodies that stood in flight. I did not know the names of these birds or the things that grew near this road. Some of the things were hairlike and vague, others were flowers that were colorless. The effect was that of stiff brushes near the road. I wished I knew the names of things. I was in presence held by them. I wished I knew the names of these things as I knew Mustang, Valiant, Charger, Dart. I walked back along another road also that lit brown. The two dogs led and wandered in place at some places. When I was near the house I had come from it was a low flat-sided building surrounded by mud and buses. Children slept in the buses. The roof of this house grew shapeless and disappeared. The walls grew rectangular and flat-sided, made of adobe. The blue mountains were painted on them, and the sun was painted on them. I passed the buses as one child was crying and his crying was as if from under water. Inside the house sixty people were awake. They drew breakfast from a huge pot. They were warm and washed. I got breakfast too. Never had a morning like this.

    A boy named Jonathan has had a bad dream. This bad dream and the way he has felt lately are making him sad, and his mood has come to the attention of Lord Sean. Jonathan woke up screaming this morning, or yesterday morning, and then he was crying. He is one of the ones who edited the film in LA. He has not said much to anyone since he got back. Now he is on a chair in the middle of a room with his hands on his knees, his knees coming apart, coming together, coming apart nervously. There is a gathering of the family like seals on their rocks, on all the surfaces of the room. Every now and then, at first, these people will ask Jonathan a question: "How did you feel about the man in the clouds? Do you think you were afraid?" But mostly they are perched in silence, and only Lord Sean is doing the talking. His kindly bulging eyes: his kindly smile. Lord Sean is the doctor and he cures the moment, whenever he can, by proceeding according to the teachings of Fritz Perls, the gestalt therapist. After seeing him in action several times, sometimes on me, I still do not know what Lord Sean is up to with this gestalt therapy, but the sessions generally ended in sobbing, expressive relief for the sufferer (or, in some cases, the wrongdoer) as he was hugged, congratulated, taken back into the Family, insane as ever but grateful at least to be back down to the level of insanity he enjoyed before his bout with Lord Sean's dread intersubjectivity.
    "All right, what was so scary about the dream, Jonathan, c'mon."
    "I don't remember," says Jonathan. Shrug, titter,

embarrassment, look around the room for sympathetic face finding. They are all sympathetic, which gives less comfort than no sympathy at all, titter, shrug.

"I say we shouldn't even help him if this is the way he's going to respond," says Nathan, the hard cop, and then the cawing of the yeasayers come down on his head: Ah, help him. Help him. Help him to open up. Jonathan doesn't know what to do. He has been apologizing, ever since this started, apologizing for letting his misery come to the attention of the others. He says "Ah, this is dumb. I mean it. I'm sorry. I appreciate what you're doing but I just don't know where to start." He wants time to work out a strategy of confession before appearing at the center of the Family's attention, but Lord Sean never lets one get away. (This takes place in a room which has come to be called the Editorial Room, because the staff of the future magazine stay here all day, amusing themselves, in the absence of any magazine to work on, by "opening up" to one another, each one hypochondriacally attentive to the subtle processes of his own mind and medically watchful over the minds of the others. Many times I would enter that room to see the same dour chess-problem faces, and someone would say, "Come on in, we're just discussing Lord Philip's difficulty in relating to Lady Samantha." or "Anthony was just telling us about some of his sex hangups. This could be groovy for your book," and an hour or two of the wildest crap would fly. And then, if the conversation had reached the peak of bitterness and wanton cruelty that most did reach, it would end in everyone saying how much they loved everybody else and somebody invariably would do a roundup speech like, "Before I came to the Family I never felt I would really *talk* about my problems. I guess that's the secret of the Family. People." And everyone would murmur, "people, people, people.") But this time Jonathan's not cooperating. He is not looking deeply enough inside himself. "I guess I'm just afraid, then," he says when someone says he's afraid, a form of defiance for Jonathan. "Maybe you're putting me uptight."

"No one's putting anyone uptight, Jonathan. We wouldn't be talking about this if you weren't already uptight. And we've been noticing it for a few days. Ever since you got back from LA as a matter of fact. . . ."

"So now you're saying it has something to do with the movie, right?" says Jonathan.

"I didn't say that," Lord Sean is relaxing into a mild self-satisfied smirk. "What are you so defensive about?"

"I'm not defensive. I just don't think it has anything to do with the film; that's all."

"Well, nobody said it did. You're the one that brought it up, Jonathan." Jonathan is not talking. Lord Sean continues: "I think you brought it up to lead us to it. I think you're crying for help when you mention the film. You want us to know something's wrong but you can't come out and tell us, so you're *leading* us to the problem. Tell us what happened when you were in Los Angeles. C'mon, something happened to you there; now what was it?"

"Jonathan, you were pretty uptight uncommunicative in Los Angeles," says Lord George, who was also there. "You were fine at work, but afterwards we couldn't get you to open up." Jonathan looks at Lord George with utter ingratitude for having pointed this out at this time.

"I think your hangup has a lot to do with Lord

George," says Lord Sean. "Something that happened between you and him in Los Angeles. Do you think ı might be right?"

"I don't know. I don't know a fucking thing. Fuck it."

"What does *that* mean, Jonathan?" says Lord Sean like a man who has been tutoring somebody and sees he will have to start all over at the beginning. "I don't think you're even trying to be honest with us, and that means you don't consider us good enough to talk to. Is that it? We're not even people to you, just objects, there when you want us and gone when you don't need us anymore. Well we are people, Jonathan, and if you can't treat us like people maybe we better not talk to you for awhile. We're not buying your uncommunicativeness." Lord Sean asks someone else about something unrelated to Jonathan. That person answers Lord Sean and they talk about this thing for awhile. Jonathan is still on his seat in the center of the room, but the conversation avoids him, bending elliptically around his head. He follows it for awhile, upset and contrite, and then he says, "Well, I'll tell you one thing, this dream I had was weird."

"What was that?" says Lord Sean, who knew he would come around. "So you feel like talking to us now. . . . Well, what about the dream? What scared you?"

"I don't know," says Jonathan, and he throws his arms around him in appalled helplessness.

"There you go again. How do you know you don't know? Are you sure you don't know? Maybe you really know."

Jonathan says, "No, I'm sure I don't know. You mean I *do* know?" Then hopefully, "Do you think I know?" At this point I leave the room and step into

[134   ]

the kitchen where a girl who has been here about a
month longer than I have sees me, gives me a tentative
quizzical smile and says: "How do you feel? Right
now?" This has happened to me before among the
Family. You are held responsible for your emotions
here, and I've been asked a few times—once while
having dinner, once right after waking up on the way
to the bathroom—to tell someone how I feel, either in
general, or sometimes, how I feel about him. Candor
is encouraged. Once, in the middle of what I thought
was a nice conversation about Boulder, Colorado, the
girl I was talking with stopped, scrutinized my face and
said, "Sometimes I want to talk to you, but I don't
know what to say." She looked worried, so I tried to
make little of it and get that problem forgotten. I said,
"Well, you're doing OK. Aren't we talking now?" She
shook her head and said, "Games," sighing, then continued to look at me, very worried about my future. I
was nervous under her stare and said, "What is it you
want to talk about?" She gave a shocked yelp, then a
laugh, as though I must be kidding. "You really think
communication is words, don't you?" she said, grabbed
my head by the ears and tossed it back and forth a
little, saying I was helpless, helpless, indulgently.
Consequently, at this time, in the kitchen, with my feelings called for, I was afraid I would be trapped in a
long lugubrious session: passion and confession; and
I said, "What's it to you?" Thought I would get a quick
glass of water and split, but Sir William, who was also
in the kitchen, said, "No, Mark, tell her how you feel.
What are you being so defensive about?" I drank a
glass of water to stop expectation, looked from him to
her, evasive, dull-eyed and went away. I go back to
the Editorial Office. Jonathan is standing in the middle
of the floor, holding his chair above his head, screaming

and panting helplessly, as though fending off some giant's attack. "I hate you dream! Fuck you, dream! Aah! I don't believe in you; you're not even there! You're nothing! Aah!" On their rocks, the seals were awestruck. A real gestalt.

"Now how about that man in the clouds!" Lord Sean suggests when Jonathan has run out of taunts for his dream and is standing quietly, the chair becoming heavier and heavier in his hands.

"I don't know who you are," says Jonathan to the man in the clouds. "You look like a cartoon figure but I can't place you." His voice and eyes seem to be warning this invisibility that he, Jonathan, is not taking it any more. "I don't know why I was afraid of you . . . I admit I was . . . I guess I was. But I don't know why . . . but . . ." It is not coming to him.

"What about from now on?" says Lord Sean.

"But from now on, I'm not afraid of you. From now on I can beat you. I can see you, and you know what I'm talking about. You're not going to harm me. I know that because you're only a dream. You can't harm me." He went on like this, expelling dreams and cloud men from his mind until he felt he was repeating himself too often; then he stops, puts down the chair and sits in it. "Well?" he asks Lord Sean. Lord Sean says, "I don't know. I think you're still keeping something from us." Jonathan starts to protest. "But you're not ready to tell us yet," says Lord Sean. "I thought you might be ready but you're not. We'll let you decide when you are. We can't waste our time helping you if you won't be honest with us." Jonathan's hands are on his knees again, and his knees are going apart, coming together, going apart again nervously. He doesn't know where he went wrong, but he knows that to mention this not knowing will open the door to the corridors of infinite regression, and Lord Sean will take him through not-knowing to not-knowing to not-knowing, poking fun and prodding through not-knowing to not-knowing. So Jonathan, continuing the tremors of his legs, says apologetically, "I think I learned a lot today. I really do."

Lord Sean is relentless in his love, though. "You *think* you learned a lot? You mean you don't know? Do you *know* you *think* you learned a lot today, or do you just *think* you think you learned a lot today?" And then he says, "Holy cow!" derisively. The touch of the poet.

When almost everyone is cleared out of the room, and Lord Sean is back at work on his novel about a group just like the Family, and Nathan is painting a table with swirls and blotches of colors, not to make it look ugly but because we have to soften our environment and become a part of it, as animals in nature, camouflaged and at home, and a man with a moustache is trying on hats, first the explorer's hat, then the football helmet, then the merchant marine cap, I ask Lord Sean if he doesn't feel himself to be a real asshole. He says he does not, but (stops typing) he welcomes the opportunity to discuss with me how I feel—really feel—about him. I will tell him, I say, but first I want to know why he played so long with Jonathan's head. He says, "I wasn't playing with his head. You're playing with *my* head. Everything we discussed here today was necessary to discuss. Not just for him, but for all of us. We're all one person. I can't play with his head because I know if I play with his head it is just like me playing with my own head. Things are too important for that. Ask him. Ask him, *he* knows what we were doing. And it wasn't me. I do most of the talking, because I like to talk, but anyone can do all of the talking, anyone

[137]

who wants. It wasn't me. What I said we all said. Even he said what I said because there's no difference between him and me; we're both one person. That's why we love each other so much, because loving each other's like loving ourselves, and we do love ourselves. Ask him if he minds what we said to him today. He won't mind, because he knows we only did it out of love." Later, I saw Jonathan alone. He was constructing a table, cutting the wood with a power saw. I asked him if he was pissed at the way he had been treated. He said, "No, they were doing that because they love me. Like I love them." He said, "Loving them's just like loving myself, because they're all me and I'm them."

Lord Byron. Lady Maya told me that before she ever met Lord Byron he used to ask about her, and word would reach her that all over town Lord Byron was asking about her when she was living in town; or when she was living in the mountains in a mansion with a rock and roll band, people used to drop by and say Lord Byron wanted to meet her. "Well," she said, "I didn't really want to see him at first. I guess I was even scared, a little turned off, you know. That happens a lot. Chicks either turn on to him right away, or they don't like him at all. I thought he was a little creepy. I didn't want him talking about me—I didn't know how he even knew me—I was scared. Then the band left and I was in that big house, alone, I don't know, I started dreaming about him. I dreamt we were talking and it was very peaceful. I saw him really clear, you know, but I don't know how I did, because I'd only really seen him once, and I never really talked to him, you know, not really. But then I realized he was plugging into me, making my head dream about him. He's really a spiritual man; that's the way a lot of the chicks first got turned on to him . . . he just plugs into their heads, like. Then I really wanted him, I just wanted him. I wanted to make it with him. I was really nervous, like walking around in that big house just wanting to see him. Then one day after I dreamt about him all night, who should come to the door but Lord Byron." Lady Maya said she came back with him to the Family that night and she has had no desire to leave since then. She told me that twenty of the girls in the Family came in because of Lord Byron. She said, "Byron was the first really real man I ever made it with. He was the first one who could make me feel like a real woman. . . . Not that it is a sex trip . . . it's more like a head trip. He just really smooths your head out . . . like, he *knows,* he really *knows.*" Lady Maya told me that she was very fucked up and she had a lot of hangups, which she can't really recall any more, and she remembered how Lord Byron told her all about her hangups as though he could read her mind. She said it happens the same way with all the chicks. Sometimes she and other women of the Family would hear the story of a girl who had just met Lord Byron and I would watch them beaming tearfully, while the new girl told how he had made her feel like a woman and how he had really really known about all her hangups, and a closeness of feeling developed among all the women who had met Lord Byron, and they sometimes sounded like women who have the same doctor.

Lord Byron is a mild-mannered sweetly smiling man of about thirty-five years, a short black man who doesn't seem to be particularly intelligent but he is, and his face and manner are of a man who is very kind. He likes to speak aphoristically. I have never heard him utter an aphorism that would not have been better said as a simple sentence, but it is nevertheless a great pleasure to hear his aphorisms. Sometimes he struggles with some sentiment he has almost lost by raising it to the poetic level of speech, and listeners wait to hear how he will balance the opening bombast ("Sometimes a man's true meaning is. . . .") as though waiting for a delicious surprise to be placed on their tongues. Usually, before speaking to a large group of people, Lord Byron likes to say, "Shucks, I ain't a big speech-maker or anything," which he is not, and he stumbles a lot when he talks to the assembled Family because he does not want to say anything haphazardously which might be unworthy of the faith they have in him. He is a man attempting to lead a responsible and spiritually consistent life and be of service to people. His intuitions and his good will have gathered around him this large group of disciples and lovers (husbands and wives) who see in him their only chance to survive the approaching destruction of America, and who even now feel themselves to be survivors, whose lifework is to find others to rescue. All the activities and projects of the Family, in a sense that they are constantly aware of, are supposed to further this rescue work, and the Family looks to Byron for the word on how this is to be done.

In Taos, people who are not in the Family, even communards on other communes, often discuss the Family in terms of the Charlie Manson family, because of the warlord quality of Byron's position, the disciple-ship of the rest and the secretiveness which is practiced toward the outside world. I heard in Taos a lot of talk that the FBI had investigated Lord Byron after the Tate killings to determine whether there was anything to worry about. Speculative thought in Taos: "First: do you really think if Lord Byron told them to kill someone they would do it? And second: Do you really think it would be so impossible for them to find someone they wanted to kill?" Many hippies of the neighborhood are titillated by this kind of thought, living so close to a potentially criminal group. The Family, it is known, is armed with rifles and hand guns, and they have four radio-controlled cars in which they patrol the streets of Taos at night, on vigilante duty, to protect local hippies from Chicanos. But Lord Byron is not Manson; his care over the people he meets is grandfatherly. At the Family, most of the women want to have children. The ones that are pregnant look forward to bringing new children into the Family, though they may not know who the biological father is. The children are cared for by all the women of the Family, and they sleep together on two buses parked in the yard. When the Family is able to dine together, everyone stands after dinner in a circle and women with babies hold them so everyone can see them, and the whole Family sings to each one. The older children jump on Byron's back and Byron walks all over the house, yelling, "Hold on! Hold on!" kissing all these pretty women, who all want to have children in the Family.

People at the Family, when telling about their former lives whether as fags (Homosexuality is not acceptable to the family. Lord Byron says, "We are not ready for that monkey business yet.") or Vassar students, usually assumed the half-ashamed and half-astounded tone that cured alcoholics use when they remember to others the extravagances of their disease.

[141   ]

Often, they used their own past selves as examples for some disgusting characteristic they found in the person they were speaking to, saying, "I used to be just like you, till I found out how it was really just making me miserable. I used to think like you, but it was just bullshit, of course, when you learn what the Family can teach you." Or they used their own lives to help you through induction fatigue, telling how this and that lesson had been a hard one for them to learn, too, but that you would certainly get over this stage of doubt, as everyone had. But they did not generally like to talk about the lives they had led in other places, other moods, and, except when asked about what had led them to join the Family (which was the single favorite topic of exchange), would refuse to speak of their other lives as though they were bad highway collisions they had anecdotalized too often. Most of them were contemptuous of the people they had been and pitied their old friends who were still that way. Letters from old friends were read aloud at night, and these letters told the listeners just how debased and destroyed were these old friends, and the verdict from the sixty tightly packed ones was always, "Better tell him to come to the Family, before it's too late!"

Lord Sean said he was once an intellectual, but now he feels all the data of his senses (Lord Sean had a scientific edge in a lot of his speech, even though he hated intellectuals) through his emotions. The story of his life, and according to him the story of what must be the life of every intellectual at the present time, was that while at college, in despair though not knowing he was in despair, he started using drugs. Lord Sean (at that time his name was Billy or Bobby) used marijuana, psychedelics, speed, and cocaine. He thought they were expanding his consciousness, and even now he acknowledges the very valuable lessons one can learn from drugs, but actually he was pilfering his mind and will in small packets until they both were gone, as he now tells it. This went on and on. Lord Sean was Bobby and he thought he was "some kind of intellectual" and he "sailed through his courses" without "cracking a book" and all the time he was "in despair" though he "didn't know it," and all the time he was "cracking up." In any case, fogged as he was, Bobby got himself married and entered some university in the graduate school of psychology, where he was working toward his Ph.D., supposedly, but was in fact too morose to care, until his wife gave birth to a son or daughter, whom Lord Sean still holds in the highest regard for not being born an acid mutant, after which he was absolutely destroyed, taut between acid flashback and acid flashback, a father and a student, bored out of his mind and prone to long fits of twenty-four-hour sleeping. This period of what Lord Sean calls the "intellectual life style" culminates in the after-dark attempted stabbing of his wife by Bobby and subsequent kidnapping of his little son or daughter, with whom he hid out in the mountains around the college. "So," he says, "I learned my lesson. You're never as smart as you think you are."

Lord Sean was still hiding in the mountains when he met the Family, which was passing through during the nomadic period before settling in Taos. His sister was already in it, and he met Lord Byron, who turned him on to many amazing things, among them that we are all god. The rest of the Family convinced him he could not find happiness in graduate school or monogamy, so Sean gave the baby back to his wife and left town with the Family. His wife and he still correspond; she and the baby and a new husband are at another commune, somewhere in Canada, and Lord Sean is trying to get them all to come to the Family.

I met a sad man today in the Tihuana Taco who said he promised once to provide whatever his parents desired, but he let them down and finally they sued him. Meeting them every day in court was hard for him. He didn't know what to say. Finally, he won the case, but he could feel his father's eyes on his back as he left the courtroom with his lawyer, and his mother was crying helplessly. He says he has tried every way of reconciliation, which is all he desires, but they do not respond to him.

Last night, after dinner, which was eaten in the house in town, all of us together, signifying that some special communication was to be made to the Family, Lord Byron, wearing his knitted skullcap, sitting cross-legged in front of the fireplace, pulled his hands out of the slash pockets of his dacron windbreaker and held up two fists: "These is fists," he said. "The rich man invent 'em so he can wash his hands without gettin' his money wet." He held them up for a while, smiling and giving everyone time to appreciate that grasp was implied in thrust, and to draw what conclusions they would from his display. Lord Byron said the move had been expensive, the magazine was expensive, and there are sixty of us now, and the Family is out of money. "I guess the time come for us to make a little requisition of funds from our friends in Reno," he said. Everyone laughed. Learned later, by asking, that Byron's been to Reno four times already and every time except the last he has won. The time before last, he went with $60 and came back with $12,000, on which money the Family has been living since then. Byron thinks the reason he lost last time is because the others told some people outside the Family where he was going and what he was doing, and the confusing telepathies of all those people muddied the air above the endeavor, causing him, though he was miles away, to make mistakes and think unclearly. This time he is asking for discretion. Wants everyone to go about his daily work and not think particularly about him, but if he should happen to cross their minds, it would help if they emitted positive, confident vibrations, which are so important. "We're with you, brother," said Sir Richard, and there were similar affirmations from around the room where we were listening to Byron in three semicircles, on the floor, on the low tables and standing up. Then Lord Byron said there was another reason he wanted to speak to us. He said, "I guess I'm sorta the leader of this group or somethin', I don't know, or people *call* me the leader, the president, the king, that's all ridiculous anyway. And I had a good time bein' the leader." I looked around the room. No one seemed puzzled or stunned, no one looked at anyone but Byron, everyone was silent and attentive. "But it's gettin' a little hard for me to be the leader, and anyway I got other things to do, so I'd like to stop bein' the leader." I expected there to be protests of some kind, but there were not, although Lord Byron has been their leader for three years, and he brought most of them here, and they have always said, at all times, "Ask Byron what to do," but everyone did reach for the ones nearest himself and without looking at them put his arms around them, always staring at Byron. "I'll be in Reno a week," said Byron, "then I'll be back. But when I get back I'm not gonna be no leader. Where's Christopher?" He looked into the dark room. Christopher, who is the man who drives the Family bus, came out of the crowd. He was smiling, but he was confused. Byron took his skullcap off, put it on top of Christopher's head, and moved it around until it looked right. "You're the leader now, Christopher. You're a Leo." Christopher said nothing, then he declined. Byron would not allow him to decline. They talked together for a while, standing still with their foreheads touching, then Christopher accepted, saying, "Well, I hope I do a good job. I don't know how I can but I guess I will," then, seeming to feel it unacceptable to continue in a casual manner, said gravely and, as many things are said in the Family, with a sense of the historical importance of the utterance, "I ask you for your help. I ask all of you. I know I am sometimes weak. I try to be strong. I ask you, help me be strong. I need your help." There was silence. Christopher looked at each face. Then, as if in response to a sudden total comprehension of these matters of official ceremony, he asked formally "Nathan, will you help me?" And Nathan, from the crowd, said, "I will help you, Christopher." "Samantha, will you help me?" said Christopher, building momentum and with tears welling in his eyes. "I'll help you, Christopher," said Lady Samantha. And he asked this question of several people whose faces he saw in the group. They all responded with dignity, showing none of the embarrassment most people feel when they are called on to speak out in a group.

After this, members of the Family who were not yet titled but who were due, were given their honors: "Rise, Sir William. Rise, Lady Lilly." Etc.

That night at bedtime, Byron's easygoing abdication was not discussed very much, though it was certainly on everyone's mind. Lady Heather said, "Lord Byron is just afraid we're getting too dependent on him. He wants to test us. He doesn't think we know how to act without him telling us what to do. He'll see. We've learned a lot." The others were all convinced that whatever had been done was necessary and, though they were uneasy about it now, it would work out for the best.

I said I read once the face is a meat jewel.

Lady Leah said, "What did you *feel,* once?"

I said, "What are you talking about?" though I was already aware that the distinction between the intellect and the emotions was being held against me again, and that Lady Leah, with whom I had spoken only once in the time I was there, had detected an inauthenticity in my bearing which she desired now to make me aware of, for, as the exhilaration in her face, which anywhere but in the Family might have been interpreted as the thrill of the kill, made plainly clear to everyone, Lady Leah was "being honest" with me. Earlier in the day I had seen her under attack from Lord Sean and his gang of therapists precisely for failing to be honest about her feelings toward Christopher, by whom she was visibly repulsed and whom she was disgusted by the thought of having touch her, but to whom she had kept saying, "I don't think I'm ready to relate to you, Christopher." The vague words were said with such a tremor of despair and brokenness that Christopher had not known at all what to make of them, especially as Lady Leah also had said, "I love you, remember that. I really do." *Love* being the absolute minimum which one extends toward any other in the Family, as *courtesy* is in lower associations of society.

[147   ]

At that time, Lady Leah had been reduced to tears by Lord Sean's expert probing at the roots of her unease, and especially when told that she had been noticed, over the past several days, and that Lord Sean had been waiting for an opportunity to tell her she was not fooling anyone but herself. That is, she did *not,* as anyone could see and as everyone had made note of, love Christopher, or anyone else in the Family, and that furthermore, it was unnecessary for her to profess love she did not feel, that she could let it come on her naturally and not feel constrained to emote, and that, most of all, she must stop her dishonesty and be sure, in the future, for her benefit and the benefit of the entire Family, to express exactly her feelings ("your honest-to-god true feelings" said Lord Sean, so that even a child could understand) toward each and every fellow Family member who should come under her scrutiny. Lady Leah had weighed Lord Sean's advice a whole day, examining the possibilities these new rules for the game afforded her, and at night, listening to me speak against ecology, and after having tried two or three times unsuccessfully to insert herself into the conversation, and after having heard me note books she had not read, for they were neither books in social work, her field of study at college, nor *Stranger in a Strange Land,* Lady Leah rose from her back to her knees, made her hands into fists which she put at her sides on the floor, and rocking on her haunches from fist to fist, said, "What did you *feel* once, Mark?" and then, after my question as to her meaning, which she had never answered, said, "Shall I tell you what I feel?" I waited at her mercy, silently praying, "Go easy, go easy," but all these things were working on her and she said, "I hate you, Mark. I hate to hear you talking. I hate your face, especially when you smile. I hate your eyes. I hate your meaningless dishonest expression whenever you look at me. I hate you. That's how *I* feel!" She stared me full in the face and her whole face was thrown forward and was full of excitement and freshness, like someone who loves to feel rain on his face and thrusts it forward to soak up the spray.

Despite the fact that I am not used to being spoken to in this way, except when the speaker is someone who loves me and therefore has good reason to feel such a depth of hate for me, I was not stunned by Lady Leah. I knew she was ready for long soggy Family hours picking with me through the little bits of our feelings, Lady Leah's and mine, for one another. I saw that the sorrowful solitary face she had worn since she had, so indelicately, spurned Christopher, had brightened and her eyes were excitedly darting all over the room, as though someone had quickly pulled two pieces of tape off her eyeballs and they bulged in the direction of their loss, and I was also aware that in the tradition of such things in the Family, after the arduous gestalt, Lady Leah and I must have together, careful, painful, and dull, and to which her hate for me was the most direct invitation, there was no other course but for us to fuck. And so, seeing these things and not being able to stop seeing these things, I was also not able to muster a concise, gut reaction to her words. Gut response, not lucid amusement, is of course what was called for in the situation, and I realize how infuriating I must have been, puffing on a pipe, lazily stoned (they knew at the Family that I stuck wads of hash in my mouth and sucked myself stoned on the sly) listening for more from Lady Leah watching with foggy eyes, growing impatient with childlike desire to finish what I had been saying about faces and jewels, and then, as all of us seemed to be stuck and dead-ended there, at the back of Lady Leah's hate, and I was still anxious to say what I was saying, I mumbled, "Sorry you feel that way," and turned to Sir William, thinking I would continue our conversation, but saw on Sir William's face, Sir William and I being friends, the look of despair men have when their dogs kill the neighbors' hens and I was the dog and love was the hen and Sir William thought they would have to put me to sleep. Already Lady Leah was on her feet and her face was flush against my ear, going, "Oooo! Rrrr! Mmmm! You've *never* had a feeling in your *life,* have you! You're incapable of feeling!"

Sir Richard, all this time, had been lying in a sleeping bag with his head in the closet, feeling and touching himself as people sometimes do after a shower or when their clothes are just off. He was caressing his chest in light circular rubs, dipping into the pit of his arm, which was raised and on which his head was resting, and clasping himself casually but firmly all down his front. Sir Richard had recently been given a haircut and, like most of the Family haircuts (too short at the sides and uneven at the top), it made him look as though his head were in a vise. In his reverie, Sir Richard's intense blue eyes had been half closed and I could tell by the oceanic rumbling and splash that came and went with his breath that he was cradling a growing quantity of spit in his mouth. "*Now* what are you going to say?" said Sir Richard, sitting straight up, opening his eyes wide and spitting on his chin and chest, which embarrassed him and me. "Hah? Hah?" he kept asking, staring me in the eyes with the hope that I would stare him in the eyes and not watch him wipe himself off. Lady Leah burst into tears, saying, "What's *wrong* with you!" to me, and Sir Richard, nodding yes, yes, said, "Tell her, Mark. How do you feel about what she just said? Look at her, don't be afraid. She's a person! We're all *people,* you understand, people!"

I told Sir Richard it was none of his business and that I would answer Lady Leah in a second, but Lady Leah disallowed, saying, "No, Mark, Sir Richard is me and I'm Sir Richard." I laughed. I was very nervous, as though I were under arrest in a foreign country, alone, and ignorant of the language, and I only wanted to convince everyone in the room of my good will and friendliness, and so I began to search myself in earnest for an exact and true description of the way I felt then, and had felt when attacked, felt toward Sir Richard and toward Lady Leah. I wished so strongly that this misunderstanding between myself and them had been avoided that I began to assume the guilt for its occurrence. I said, "All right, you're right . . . let me think about it." Then I stated tenatively, "Well, I felt annoyed, I guess. I felt hurt, too." I was thoughtful, academic; surprisingly, at that time, it did not occur to me that I was doing a shameful clownlike thing, placating these people to preserve myself. I felt I was being commendably cooperative to the rules of a group I admired and was a part of. I looked at their two faces, Richard's, righteously angry and poor Leah's, swollen and damp, which had so terrified and appalled me a moment ago, and I wanted them to know how important they were to me. "Please," I said, "why did you say that to me, Lady Leah? What have you noticed about me?"

But Lady Leah couldn't think of anything and was panting like a moving man against the wall, having heaved off her load so recently and resting from her exertions. Sir Richard, jutting forward his jaw and sitting now with his knees high at the sides of his head, the vise for which his haircut was a perfect fit, and his fingers interlocked with his toes, which he had spread wide, was angrier than ever at me and said, "I don't think you *were* hurt by what she said, you know that? I think you think you *should* have been hurt, but I don't think you *were* hurt, because I don't think you have any real feelings, yet." At that time contriteness left as easily as it had come upon me, like the loss of harmony, and I felt again the need to escape this strange self-indulgent fanaticism. Sir Richard's face was full of the religious fervor, so alive and insane, which I had seen him aspire to but never attain at the after-dinner hugs and sings each night when he was either choirboy pious or frankly bored except when in the exercise of what had practically become his official duty at the Family—initiating the group response to something Lord Byron or some other speaker had said. That is, if Lord Byron said, "I hope you'll all pray for me," and then paused, it would invariably be Sir Richard, staring into the fireplace and speaking as though to spirits someone had called from another world, who said, "We'll *all* pray for you, brother," or "You can count on me," which the rest of the Family would then repeat or embellish at first in voices scattered and alone, then more or less in a group bark. At this time Sir Richard looked like a malicious, small monkey. We argued for a while. I called him names at first and then attempted to insult him by describing him. I am usually good at this, and though it is a disgusting way to act I do act this way. The precisest character assaults did not make Sir Richard unhappy, though, or make him stop pressing his face closer and closer to my own, like a giant balloon I came upon once in a dream. In response to whatever I said to him, he said, "Good! I'm *glad* you called me that! I learned something about myself!" implying he had a kind of courage I obviously lacked. "At least I'm getting you to be honest!" he said, turning each of my words into a success for himself in some area of accomplishment which I was not able to grasp. And, though each of my remarks was designed only to end the scene with him, and though I often stopped altogether, satisfied I had said all that had to be said, he would press his face closer, lopsided and firm, and say, "Go on! Go on!" so pleased to be spoken of, in any way that he forgot Lady Leah's prior demands on me. Lady Leah noticed and became annoyed. She was no longer sobbing but then went through a series of exaggerated, expressive mimes: petulance, fury, boredom. Sir Richard did not see her, because he held his face as still as someone who is having his portrait painted for the first time and doesn't know if he should move his eyes.

Lady Leah left, aloof and alone, and I couldn't think of anything to tell Sir Richard, toward whom I did not feel close. I was discouraged: there were no thoughts in my head; I felt unkind. Sir Richard sensed the loss of interest all around him, I suppose, and rose to his feet telling me to look at him. I was lighting my pipe. He said, "I know what you're doing with that pipe, Mark. Look at me! You can't even look at me!" He was right. I continued to play around with the pipe, which hung from my teeth like a skyhook and which had a little tin cover to keep out the wind, and which I do not now have, because Sir Richard, who had not felt good for a couple of days, since his haircut and the suspicion that his role on some Family project was not appreciated as much as it should be, both of which came on the same day, and who was now furious at me, saying "Look at me!" swiped it out of my mouth and sent it across the Editorial Office into a corner where it broke its neck and started a small fire among some letters addressed to Dear Advertiser and opening with: "Taos, New Mexico. The sun, the land, the new people experimenting with the New Life." I got the pipe and stepped on the fire, then returned to where Sir Richard was still standing, and sensing that he was now afraid I would hit him, told him, in a taunting and degrading manner, not to be afraid, that I would not hit him, all the time looking as though I was about to and feeling strongly the desire to. "Well?" he said. "Well?" as though to say, "Here I am, naked and honest, and I've shown you what it is to *really* feel emotion. Now what are you going to do about it? Hit me?"

Sir William, who had been sitting in a chair throughout this scene, his impassive kindly face watching none of it, looked up from a book he was reading, a text on scientology describing the use of the E-meter, when he heard Sir Richard knock my pipe across the room. He sensed that something was going wrong with the gestalt of the situation. "Take it easy, Sir Richard," said Sir William. This was all he meant to say, and he immediately resumed his reading, but Richard began explaining his position to him, saying, "Mark is trying to evade me," and showing how everything he had done to that point was the correct procedure, as could be determined from the common law Family slogans: Our business is people. We are all gods. I love him and he loves me. And we are the losers who decided to be winners. Sir William said, "Well, maybe he doesn't *want* to confront you now. Maybe he's tired." Sir Richard, who was at this time not near me in the room and had relaxed enough to continue to familiarize himself with his body, was holding his buttocks in his hands as though they were somebody else's, somebody he was helping to climb into a loft. He looked at me in a distant, haughty, pretentious way which it happens he was copying from my own recent looks at him and said, "Him? He loves it! He's interested!" I said I was not at all interested. He spoke louder and louder, saying, "You *are* interested! This is the most interesting moment of your life. And why?" He was pressing and releasing, pressing and releasing his buttocks easily and regularly, in a cow-milking rhythm. "Because *I'm* the first person you've ever met who's *honest* with you! You're fascinated. You *love* it!" Then some people whom Sir Richard was keeping awake with his screaming came into the room, relaxed themselves on all the surfaces, and began the lengthy process of finding out what was *really* meant and *really* felt by him and by me and themselves, dividing the mind and the world into too-small components, because delicacy of analysis is their pride the way miniaturization is the pride of the Japanese and losing the pieces in their minds, getting stuck, being wrong, breaking into other subdivisions of accusation and argumentation among themselves, all gods, all earnestly creating the psychology and vocabulary of gods. All of them, Sir Richard, Sir William, and Lady Leah and all the rest were in a very good mood, and on several occasions people cried with joy at having some personal insecurity or insufficiency explained to them by the others.

The next day I was sick. I felt I was stranded in all this yellow dust with maniacs and yet I felt I couldn't leave because there was no survival outside the Family. As for my sickness, I didn't know what it was; I was nauseous and tired, unable to eat. I spent the day on the floor in my sleeping bag watching the bustle and excitement in the room they had called Central Control where they were promoting their movie, calling booking agents, writing ads. Watching them perform their functions with the cheerful energy of any

New York bullshit agency, plugging their giant map with colored pins as each new booking was arranged, I felt at the same time that I was able to see through them and could catalog their flaws, and that I was a part of them, unable to detach myself, unable to imagine any reality outside the Family. There is so much wrong with this place, I thought. They're all like any people caught in any fad, fooling themselves putting on an act. I lay back with my arms behind my head, looking and looking, and nausea like balloons filled with liquid flopped from place to place in my stomach. I didn't know if I could leave the Family.

And this is the thing that is unimaginable to people who have never been in a place like this, experiencing in concentrated and ceaseless insistence a single vision of life, even for a short time, without any exposure to outside information—the newspapers, movies, friends from other places—to reinforce the conflicting, scrambled ideas of the world developed in growing up in America. I was not sure any more that the real world was actually, as I had always been sure it was, relative, meaningless, a matter of curious interest and full of all possibilities and allowances for any way or style of living. Now I had serious doubts: What if the world was as they said, doomed to annihilation except for the Family itself? This had been explained to me, over and over, coherently, believably, inescapable result of a population realizing and respecting no absolutes except power, and while at first whatever they said to me I took in the spirit of hearing someone's interesting rap, the consistency of what was said and its appeal to the desire for things to finally in some way be meaningful, for life and death to be definable, and also the daily influence of the life these people had created, which was incredibly full of love and a closeness to each other

I have always assumed was impossible, all this had at last made me afraid to leave them. Even though in my thoughts I thought they had created a communal insanity that was for some reason dangerous, I had become similarly insane and felt that life away from this place would be full of despair. And while I could see that this one was a fool and that one was fooling the others, still it is a fact that at the Family they lived all the time at a level of intensity unapproachable anywhere else, and that even living cramped and in squalor, eating poorly, they were higher than I have been on acid, reeling and weeping, laughing, insanely and incredibly necessary to one another, and best of all they had changed themselves and been reborn, and I thought, that is it, that is what I am most afraid of, to lose myself, not be who I am, to be changed. How can I leave?

All this thing about the Family, so unkind and distant, has been written while I was not there any more—from the outside—and it shows their faces and bodies doing this and that, and I realize the place looks just foolish sometimes in my writing, the way if you saw a movie of these people yelling at one another over dreams and hugging one another after dinner you could say, "What is wrong with them?" and not understand the values that will cause people to give up all comforts and all they own, their names and clothes and the old sense of themselves that they have built up to protect themselves in America, and try, try to subordinate the desires of their moments to the wishes of the group. That is hard for me to understand also, from the outside, but then it was clear to me that they must do what they are doing if only because it is one of the ways we have been forced, very recently, to find means of divergence from what has come to be normalcy in America, where we have been raised to be competitive, envious, alone, and never to conspire, and where we have been raised to be reasonable and reasonably to act for self-gain, and where at last a lasting concern of each one for himself has come to harden into what he himself completely is. At that time, when I was sick and wanted to get away and yet wanted to stay, all the magic seemed to be on their side, all the world was visible to me through the metaphors of their language, and I felt that leaving would be going away into the unknown, although I would only be returning to America, which was not unknown but was known very well. That is how enthralled I was, and how much a part of them, although I do not believe in things usually and dislike belief and distrust it.

But I said, "I'm sick and I have to get some good food to eat," so I got out of my sleeping bag and went outside into Taos, down the street into a drug store where I had eggs and coffee and pie and read the papers. Then I was going to go back, but I thought, maybe I'll see my friend Eric for a while, and I went over to see Eric at his gallery where he was sitting outside typing, and we talked about the Family, which he berated and reviled with great hilarity, and which I then berated and reviled as well, having a good time, telling about the unbelievable fight I had had the night before, making the whole thing funny. Then I was going to go back, but Eric suggested that since I was sick I should spend the night at his chick Suzy's house outside town. He drove me there; we sat around smoking hash, and I was cynical and comfortable. The next day I thought I would go back but I didn't, and the day after that the same, and when I thought of the Family I felt I had failed, failed to remake myself into a new person. Every day I didn't go back, soon amazed that I had ever been there.

Got a ride to Santa Fe, then took a bus to Albuquerque. On the bus two Indians were speaking in a language I didn't understand. The bus driver let them off by the side of the road at some placeless vista of yellow dust, and said something to them in that language. From downtown Albuquerque I got a limousine to the airport. The driver told me a story about a rich woman from New York who had gotten into his limousine at the airport and wanted to be driven all the way to Taos. On the way, she told him her daughter was staying on a commune there and she had come to persuade her to go back to college. The woman was very upset, the driver said. Kept asking his advice, though he told her it was none of his business. In Taos, they asked around and found the commune was several miles outside of Taos. The woman wanted to go there. The driver had to charge her extra. He said when they arrived at the commune, name of which he couldn't remember, the daughter was surprised and not pleased to see her mother. He said the girl seemed healthy enough, and she was clean. He was surprised she was wearing clothes, but she was. The mother begged and pleaded. She told the daughter she did not understand. She said she would do anything if the daughter would come back home. Everyone was sad with her gone. But the girl said she was happy there and would not return to New York. The woman even pleaded with the driver to help convince the daughter, but the driver said it was none of his business. The girl would not go. Finally the mother gave up. The driver saw her give the girl a lot of money, which the girl refused at first but then put in her pocket. The mother got back in the limousine and he drove her back to the Albuquerque airport. She was crying the whole ride. She kept saying she didn't understand. He told her, sure, kids like to go out on their own. He said he had wanted to go out on his own when he was a kid, but he had not done it, and now he wished he had. He told her he was not happy. He said he was glad the girl was doing what she wanted to do.

I took a plane to Los Angeles, where the sun was setting through raspberry, orange and black arcs above the city. From a bus heading into west LA I saw the poem of Los Angeles, which is a beautiful woman at the wheel of an avocado Porsche, crying and blowing her nose, with Kleenex balled up between her thighs.

Berkeley

At home in the home of revolutionary fervor, where Rateyes has a little room, mattress on the floor, surrounded by posters of the Indian chiefs and post cards of optical illusions, portraits of the Surrealists as young men in Paris and as old men standing in front of the Museum of Modern Art on 53rd Street; surrounded by all the little appliances: flour sifter for his grass, box of illustrations and X-Acto knives and mucilage for making cutouts. Rateyes said several months ago he was coming out here to see Charlie Manson, but since then very heavy shit has come down and Rateyes says he has been getting himself together in preparation for the massive government oppression we all expect in a few months, a few weeks. Things are not well. He was busted with grass on Telegraph Avenue and now he cannot be seen there after dark or he will be busted again. When he has to cross the Avenue to get somewhere at night, he races across the street at top speed and disappears down a side street. Everyone I talk to says the stock market is about to crash and that this will lead to a military takeover of the government. Rateyes' brother says this coup actually took place during Eisenhower's second term. A man finds out about it after he has been elected President. Rateyes' brother invites me to look at some photos of Kennedy before and after a certain date, the day he was told he is a puppet of the military and these pictures are very convincing.

Shotguns and I.D. Rateyes called a meeting of his house on the feasibility of everyone chipping in for a shotgun. The assault today by New York construction workers on demonstrating high school kids; National

Guard killing of four in Ohio; Rateyes is certain the shit is coming down. It is coming out in the open. "I say it's just this. You have to decide, that's all, when they come to your house looking for you, do you just go with them, go to jail for twenty years, getting tortured every day, getting fucked over, or do you fight? That's all. Everything else is bullshit. If you don't decide on that, fuck it, you just don't have any idea." Rateyes is generally in a good humor these days, doing plenty of cocaine, working all night on cutouts and thank you letters to his uncle, who has sent him money. His brother thinks it is bullshit to write the old man a letter (he has gotten some bread, too), but Rateyes calls him up to say the time is coming fast when they will need all the help they can get.

Everywhere everyone is thinking about the revolution. This was at first upsetting to me, having come from New Mexico where revolution is old and pitiful, out of fashion, and has been replaced by the pastoral, but soon I was just as happy to be urban and political and started reading the paper again.

In the restaurants here they sit all day, maudlin and sleepy, waiting for riots to pass by in the streets, and Rateyes' brother says every Saturday he goes to a shooting range outside Berkeley with a carload of friends and he is learning to shoot rifles and pistols. Rateyes mimics his brother's words, sounding like a baby, says his brother will be shot down one day on his way to practice in the country. The revolutionary steps taken by either brother generally infuriate the other brother, and they subject one another's ideas and plans to rigorous scrutiny, always thinking one another to be theoretically or morally deficient. Rateyes' brother had his picture on the cover of some underground paper, sitting at a table creating bombs from little wires and clock parts. Rateyes called him up and said he should be ashamed of

[162   ]

himself for endangering his life. "What do you think this is, a *game,* man? You think the pigs are fuckin' *scared* of your fuckin' picture? What is this, man, suicide?" But Rateyes also is constantly berating himself for not being ready. "What if they come in right now? Right now. Why not right now? Who's stopping them? They'll come in here, all I have is a knife. I get two choices, either I let them take me or I stab myself. Is that power? What's wrong with me? I know it's coming, I know they have my name, like they have your name and Arthur's name and everybody's, and I'm sitting here with a little knife." But at this time all his money goes for cocaine, which is expensive (up to sixty dollars a spoon in Berkeley) and which Rateyes snorts a lot of, and he doesn't have the money to arm himself.

Rateyes and I went out walking. We were arguing about the existence of guerrilla warfare in America today. Rateyes notes there are six hundred documented cases of sabotage against government and police properties in the last five years. I do not know if this is true. I am saying there is no guerrilla war and there cannot be one because the people of the country do not like us. Rateyes insists. The empire is toppling. It is late at night. We come upon two men who are standing in a hole in the sidewalk. They are in overalls and blue caps. Rateyes asks what they are doing. They say they are fixing telephone cables that someone has burned. "Was it an accident or something?" asks Rateyes. Then he and the two repairmen break out laughing. Rateyes, who has an incredible memory for poetry and rhetorical writing says, "Well boys, as we are taught by the *Minimanual of the Urban Guerrilla,* written by Carlos Marighella, 'Today to be an assailant or terrorist is a quality that ennobles any honorable man because it is an act worthy of a revolutionary.' " The men in the hole say,

"Well, be good," and everyone is laughing. Rateyes says, "See that? Right outside my door. Elia, we have to get *ready*." But no one in Berkeley is ready for anything at this time. Most of our friends wake up at noon and get stoned by three in the afternoon, the rest of the day spent in the Mediterranean Café going from table to table looking for newspapers to read. Everyone thoroughly informed of national and international events, everyone casting around for night drugs, something to perk up lives of waiting, then, at night, doing these drugs and going over to Bongo Burger to talk about what they are on.

I cannot sleep in Berkeley. There is no room. I stay on the floor of the living room in the house where Rateyes has a little room. This room has a mother dog and her puppies, all curled asleep like lengths of hose, getting up at night to take a few steps and throw up leaving pasty acrid cookies of puke here and there all around me, and there are starving cats also living here. The cats sleep and pissed on my face and sleeping bag. I throw them across the room when I wake to find them on my face. This makes them love me and follow me around the house during the day. It is a very ugly house, full of college students who are bitter and seem hurt because Rateyes tells friends they can crash here. These people like to wake me early in the morning by bursting into the living room and cleaning it, asking me if I intend to get a job. This is incredible. Most incredible is the fact that this house is on rent strike and they are constantly whooping it up about the weekly meetings and outings of revolutionary organizations and committees they all belong to, which is an indication of the hegemony which the idea and aura of revolution has attained in this little collegiate suburb, becoming the social inertia and the status quo having places for everyone filling time, injustice and festival; mental ease of wartime—relaxing and exciting like actual combat. One particularly fat and sulky girl named April who lives on the second floor with lanky soggy Rod has said she wants me to leave because I am lazy. Says to Rateyes, "It wouldn't be so bad if your friends were really revolutionaries, but they're not. They're just these poet types sitting on their asses all day." Rateyes is always kind to this fat girl because he is worried that people cannot live together, that he, Rateyes, is not doing enough to create unity in the house, but she is intractable. Feels Rateyes' friends (I am not the first he has palmed off on these people as a "big New York radical") do not talk to her or care about her. Rateyes says they do care about her and fabricates messages to her from friends who have been here and gone. "You remember Danny? He said you're really together." Yesterday, standing stocky and curious in one of her gigantic shifts, she asked me if I stole a towel. Her friend Jane, also residing on the second floor, a thin girl who has a Harpo Marx look and sometimes looks like a line drawing of Harpo Marx, has accused me of stealing a knife and a package of stationery. I am planning to leave them with a massive crushing phone bill, which they will discuss and divide far into their old age.

Reflecting how strange it is that so much of what one considers as "oneself" disappears, evaporates, when one does not have a *home*. A place of inclusion and exclusion, where things are known and available, and the moment-by-moment passing of daily life can be taken at least a little for granted. I have been sleeping on cots, couches, floors, sleeping bags, army blankets, dirt, dust, car seats for several months and now when I say something and someone disagrees with what I have said I am the first one to agree with him. That is, there is an aspect of identity which is lost when identifiable place is lost, and the traveling self is not the self at home. I am quieter, I never think, I smile too much and for no reason, I have lost most "traits" and "characteristics" of personality which I and others have in the past known me by. I am without energy and incapable of making plans, never know the time and can never talk to someone without looking around distractedly, looking for something which I have not been able to name yet. When you are traveling, all of your ideas are in doubt.

Scene of a black man standing in the center of a ring of white people, all students, professors, radicals, on the Berkeley campus. The noon crowds. Berkeley campus is always filled with milling leisurely crowds, reading the handbills and gathering in tired globular formations to hear musicians and speakers. Generally, when there are speeches, two men appear on the roof of the student union and photograph the action in stills and movies. The crowd boos these men, and later the rest of the speeches are completely stopped when the speakers scream at the cameramen. This black man was going through the *Chronicle,* page by page, for a small circle of observers, drawing inspiration and anecdote for a series of tirades against white people. One white man tried to agree with him, saying, "Right on, brother." The black man looked at him with the look of a man who sees right through a salesman's pitch, and said: "You og-ly, dumb, sneaky, bullshit, jive, motherfuck, why don't you shut your mouth while I'm trying to talk to these people?" The man put up his palms to show he was giving in and did not say anything else.

The black man was short, mischievous, pawed the ground in a fluid in-place walk as he talked. His crowd got bigger and bigger. It amuses these people very much to be insulted. Black man said, "I never *met* a white man wasn't a honkie, full of shit, all fucked up and a liar too." Tittering from the crowd. As their interest waned they drifted away, and he was soon left alone with the *Chronicle,* shaking his head in disgust and disbelief as every page was new evidence of racism in America. "God *damn!* God *damn!"* he kept saying, overwhelmed.

Woke, almost as the sun was going down, bad-tempered and soggy, need to renew myself for the evening, read several newspapers, took a small variety of mismatched foods from the refrigerator and ate them in Rateyes' vacant room to avoid detection. What did I dream? Certain drugs are excellent for the dreams but very poor for the memory. Scott came over looking for Rateyes. Scott is a friendly male chauvinist from New York. When you are not in a good mood he is hard to talk to, because his gimmick is to stop the conversation and write down what you have just said. Later he will show you a new batch of poems, which he produces at breakneck speed, and you will recognize among them something you have told him, an anecdote from your life, now transformed, arch and poised, poetic. He showed me an Oregon driver's license and asked me if I had one, too. Someone is selling blanks for ten dollars. Rateyes has five, which he intends to use for passports. Scott and I talked for a while, put each other down about the women we have been seen with, Scott saying all his life he has been envied for the beauty of his women. This sent me from the room, groggy, with all this food in my pockets, toward the Avenue. On the

Avenue I went from bookstore to bookstore in search of chance encounters or new publications. Noticed a congestion of ecology paperbacks and books about Indians, none of which looked interesting. Went to the Med for coffee, and to find more newspapers. *San Francisco Chronicle,* May 30, 1970: Child Killer Claims Wife Lied. Los Angeles. Weeping, convicted child killer Ronald Fouquest pleaded with his common-law wife yesterday to "come forward and tell the truth" about how her five-year-old son died. Police said it was "not likely" that Mrs. Fouquest, formerly Betty Landsown, would appear. I tore this out to give to Scott, who likes to find illustrations for newspaper items and other things. He is presently looking for two pictures to illustrate the phrases Give a Shit and Take a Shit. In the Med I heard someone coughing the whole time I was there. Steve came in and told me a friend of his had almost drowned. We discussed drowning and water. People drown in water. It is not hard to understand. And yet even aware of the danger of drowning, people still swim in water. Postulate that it is the very fear of drowning itself that drives them to swim in water. Water is one of the substances in which one is least likely to drown. It is more difficult to drown in water than in almost anything else. Steve imagines a swimming pool full of oranges. He says he pictures himself diving into the pool off a high diving board. We realize that after such a dive, he would certainly drown. Once immersed in oranges it will not be easy to surface again. It would be a great deal easier in water. Likewise, pools full of any other things, nails, cotton, cement, coins, would more easily drown a diver than a pool full of water, and could also break his hands. It is because of this property of water, that it is difficult to drown in, that people swim in water instead of these other things.

And yet people are always drowning in water. We related this to the phenomenon of co-option. Steve told me he is moving to the country to meditate. He cannot meditate in Berkeley because he is bored.

At this time I remembered I was supposed to meet Rateyes at Saperstein's house. Rateyes wanted me to see some people from an anarchist commune. When I got there, Rateyes, Saperstein and Shefter, who lives with Saperstein, were discussing plans to rip off *Scanlan's Monthly*. This project, to have *Scanlan's* provide the three of them with thousands of dollars and the use of credit cards so they could do an entire issue on the existence of a guerrilla war in America at this time, had occupied them for five weeks. They no longer knew if they wanted to do it, or if it would be possible, and the subject generally caused them to lose their tempers. Rateyes still wanted to do it and kept creating the image of a young kid in Iowa or Nebraska picking up a copy of *Scanlan's,* colorful, loaded with pictures and diagrams, and quotes from the great anarchists, and saying, "Wow, it's really possible," and then showing it to his friends ("You know how these things happen," says Rateyes), and then, with his friends becoming a guerrilla cadre right there in Iowa. Saperstein, on the other hand, sees a senator rising on the floor of the Senate with his issue of *Scanlan's* in his hand, enraged and thrilled, and calling for activation of the concentration camps. "That's all they need," says Saperstein, "for us to collect a hundred pages of evidence and put it in a national magazine. Who do you think reads *Scanlan's,* Rateyes?" "I know. I know," says Rateyes, as the one thing they can all agree on is that *Scanlan's* is a pig magazine and only pigs (liberals and Jewish intellectuals) read it. Shefter says no one will care what is in the magazine, and that he, Shefter, doesn't care either. He has read a lot about guerrilla warfare and is convinced there is none in America at present. The three of them, and myself, are always posed and grotesque when we are together, like nonexistent beings struggling to come into the world ahead of each other. At this time, the show they are putting on for one another is that they are not interested in anything but the money. Keep referring to their activities as "ripoffs" though none of them has ever actually ripped anyone off, and they worry a great deal about the ways which *Scanlan's* will rip *them* off. Actually, Rateyes never worries about money, always has enough, enjoys giving small amounts of it away, but likes to appear as though he has business sense. Many people I know who are idealistic and politically radical seem to find their way into mail-order pornography, publication of sex newspapers, and other low-level exploitative capitalistic ventures out of the same urge to be "realistic" about making a living, which they always overdo. The idea here is to be perceptive and never naïve as to the lowest elements of character. . . .

Two kid anarchists came over today to talk to Rateyes and interest him in joining their group. They got up twice to leave because of such heavy insulting. One of them, Isaac, is evidently the leader of a little band, and he is incredible to watch, looking ridiculous with a bottle of whiskey in a paper bag, his nervousness raised to the level of a full-bodied deformity, attempting you can tell to be magical. He spun off a standard surrealist line, determined and unchanged since WW I, told us about "the boredom of your daily life," attacked the Panthers for being pigs and Fred Hampton for not being revolutionary enough. I asked them what they have done, what is their program. Isaac said, "We subvert reality and supersede it." I said, "But what do you do?" He said, "We subvert reality . . . [pause, letting this sink in, letting the weight of it fall upon me] and we supersede it . . . [smile, nod]." I said I needed some anecdotes. Your position is indefensible from the standpoint of any reasonable doctrine, but if you have some terrific anecdotes, things you have actually carried out, that is something respectable in itself. He said, with a feigned casualness, as though presenting something so innately exquisite it needed no embellishment, "O, we do things like talk about money to bank tellers, tell them about money. . . . We burn money in the Bank of America. . . ." Went on to relate tales of throwing melons at SDS meetings "to get them to think about the reality of their situation" and stealing a projector at a showing of "Weekend" by Godard. The fascination is in watching an imperfect bizarre Manson, a shaman who has not got his act together. He received a pitiful spirit breaking, but I told him I was definitely interested in contacting him again. Called him later on. His mother answered, said Isaac was out with his friends at Bongo Burger.

And finally, there is no reason to be here either, in this house of fat fascists posing as a commune, hoarding food, and trying to cement a languishing friendship with Rateyes built on quotes which we quote to one another, losing myself again in fashion, boring myself with the newspapers.

Wheeler's Ranch

We rode up to Wheeler's yesterday. The guy who picked us up turned out to be from the Navy. He had one of those slippery looking sports shirts on: red; pinioned a cold six-pack between his thighs, would reach down and rip another can out after chucking the empties violently out the window like a man delivering urgent messages to the landscape. He had very short hair, but seedling beard and moustache in timorous wisps of yellow like streaks of butter were growing. I asked him about this and he described a tortuous bureaucratic process of permission slips and written requests he had to undergo to grow hair in the Navy. His reason for visiting Wheeler's this time (said he had been here several times to camp out in the woods) was to arrest a deserter who, all evidence pointed out, was in hiding up at Wheeler's. He said he would certainly not bring this deserter in, unless he wanted to come, but would say he had gone to Canada. He himself, he says, has gone AWOL twice.

Along the road that serves as the central artery of the property, the appearance was of wasted, post-Civil War bleakness. Groups of people in tents of rags and plastic bags leaning together in bleary conversation, bumming cigarettes off people in passing cars. A cluster of Volkswagen campers slotted off the road near the entrance gate, a small colony whose location was determined by the vehicles' difficulty in making progress any further down the terrible rutted road, roving malcontents barely recognizing each other's presence in this little area. There are houses off the road on a downslope at this point, and one of them is supposed to be Bill Wheeler's, but we didn't go down to see it. First impressions were of immense and irreconcilable angers huddled together, small and mechanical men and women and their vehicles, rising not far out of a dust road, under a high-standing bright blue sky with occasional luxurious white reclining cloud bodies. We got out of this sailor's car and a crowd of young kids rushed us for cigarettes and change. They all had exultant pandhandler smiles, which often create envy in people who have things and who vaguely wish they were able to present themselves to other people with the clarity of panhandlers. This area was yellow and tan under the bright sun, with light explosions off the windows and hoods of the car bodies.

We came upon a small house about a mile into the canyon, set at the bottom of some earthsteps cut into the hillside. We examined this structure, which was a single room set on logs and up off the ground, walls primarily made of wooden window frames and windows, canvas flaps, and a canvas roof. It was large enough for a double bed and some floor space, a small stove and bags of food. Symbols of the transformations of the soul were stuck in between some wall slats; a huge chunky gold dollar sign, apparently some kind of belt buckle from a former existence, an astrological calendar of suede gray with white type, a photograph of a group of soldiers grouped by the side of a white barracks, three tiers of faces cocked at individual angles. The walls were also hung with fur coats of exotic furs, giving the place the look of a tent of some mountainous warring tribe. There was a plastic sink cradled in a frame of beams at the side of the house. Also boards laid out for future extensions to the structure.

Later, walking away from this house, we saw a guy coming toward us. We asked if he had built it and he said he had. His name was Obie. Obie has red hair and a beard. He wore shorts, a sweater, and a towel around his neck as he was coming from the beach. Invited us in to tell us about the house and smoke some of his grass, which he praised highly. He said the house took him two months to complete. I wanted to know if he had gotten a lot of help from the other people at Wheeler's. Said they had at first wanted to help him out, but they were so helplessly perverse in their standards of construction that after the floor was finished he walked on it and fell through. After that he asked for a cessation of aid and did his house alone. His father, also named Obie, helped. His father has been here longer than he has. He lives in a tent on another part of the ranch. Obie says his father turned him on to grass when he was sixteen. "My father lives over here . . . my mother lives over there (pointing faraway to the south, San Francisco). For twenty years I lived with my mother . . . now I'm out here. She gave me that." Adjusts the dollar-sign buckle. Obie was in the army in special intelligence, but while there, stationed in Germany, he engaged in what he calls his "revolutionary" activities. To Obie it is a revolutionary activity to smoke dope. I said, "How many revolutionaries were there besides you in the army?" Obie said, "Well, in my outfit there were thirty-eight of us, and only fourteen weren't, out of fifty-two altogether." I said, "Thirty-eight revolutionaries out of fifty-two!" He said, "Sure, we all had our stashes up there, kept stoned all the time."

Obie and I played flute duo for a while. Neither one of us plays. Then he demonstrated the progress he is making on the guitar, which he has been studying for four months. I told him I know this guy named Lester who says everyone at Wheeler's is lazy, and Obie said, "The hardest thing in the world to do is nothing. That's what I decided it was time to learn how to do. I'm retired." He is a Zen Buddhist, he told us, and spends a good deal of time examining and scoffing at the information of his senses. This information, while comprising the real world, strikes Obie as illusory. However, unlike many mystical people, the shadowy quality of substance does not anger him or make him feel like rending it forever to get at the essences that there are somewhere. He simply finds it pleasant to roll about in his head the irony of reality's pretenses. He uses as an example the color green on a leaf. "Sometimes I'll just look at the leaf for a long time, a real long time, and I begin to see that all the color green is in light waves reflected off of the leaf into my eyes and into my head. The same with the whole thing. The leaf shape and size and everything. It's all just given to us through the sense perceptions, and that could all be lies."

Obie, like many people we have met from Wheeler's, has the sense that whatever happens in the political revolution, the end result, after the shooting is over, will be the kind of life he is now leading. Obie sees everyone in America coming to the country to live. Abandoning the cities like old skins. He envisages the hillsides of this canyon studded with little cabins, full of men who play instruments.

Lester, who owns a home and nursery down the road from Wheeler's Ranch where Linda and I spent a couple of weeks, describes a visit to Wheeler's: "It's really marvelous, really. Quite fabulous in fact. The first thing you come upon, at the gate, is a huddle of children, they need twelve cents, a cigarette. Then you're walking across the land and you come upon someone in the full lotus position, absolutely motionless. But you know he's American because as you pass he waves and says 'Hi.' We used to see one fellow there we called the sun gazer. He was constantly looking straight into the sun. Subsequently of course I found out you shouldn't do that. Creates blind spots over your retina. But he was constantly facing down the sun. The sun gazer. Hmm." (It is Lester's particular choice of mannerism that he make short noisebursts after a good number of his sentences which seem to imply assent with what he has just said. This is never unpleasant for a listener, because Lester gives the impression he has somehow joined in listening to and is in fact pleased with his statement of the facts, as though he is being careful to see that each of his statements has been true enough to warrant its coming into existence.) "Then of course there's Wheeler himself, always running about with some mad scheme. Always whooping away up there. Of course he seems to think it's perfectly fine for all those people to sit around all day long, taking drugs and staring at one another in perpetuity until death, but you say to him 'Wheeler, this is a terrible shame. A waste. Can't you get these people to *do* anything.' Hmm. But no, he'll tell you they'll work when the spirit moves them. If everyone just works when he feels like it, well, everything will turn out as it should. That's all very fine, but you see some girl get up and hoe for five minutes and then sit down again because she's tired of doing it. Wheeler—Wheeler—will beam away at her, but you say, 'Wheeler, this girl hasn't done a damn thing. Not a damn thing. Hmm.'

"But I suppose this is the way they must relearn things, important things, I imagine, that have been forgotten. Americans feel so estranged from the land. Americans don't feel at home in the world, not at home in the world. That's the sad truth of it. But I don't know. You ought to be able to take care of yourself at least and not go into the world like an infant. Roughing it." Lester is always at work on his place down the road. He says, "I know the truth about this country

[176   ]

because I know what my neighbors know . . . they are the people, the working people," often speaking as though he was the spy of the Left on the common man, and saying, "And my neighbors do *not* like to see these hippies on welfare." Lester believes in work and has said, "In this meaningful work is the meaning of life," and his criticism of Wheeler's open land is that it creates tribes of leisure who will alienate the working man from the concept of socialism and who will, themselves, be lost in religious superstition and the occult. Lester says Wheeler was always a crazy kid. He has always liked Wheeler but is put off by his manner, which is to shift balletically while speaking to someone, arranging himself in contorted inorganic poses, pressing his nose with the tips of his fingers, and flicking his tongue up to his nose to lick it. When he inherited the land he was initially quite troubled about what to do with it. Kept it a secret from his hip friends. Since Wheeler opened his land, though, he has been much happier with himself, Lester notes, "Oh yes, he's in a fine mood."

June 23. We have lanterns, flashlights and candles, but nothing extends the day. Night starts with the fog that rolls in from the west at six, settles in the leaves and branches of the trees until dark, and then rains down on the tent until noon the next day. I have met someone named John who lived at the bottom of the canyon with his friend, Little Paranoid, an hour's hike from any other part of the Ranch down a steep hill. They were there because they cannot stand the crowds on the land, and Little Paranoid was bitten on the neck by some chick at one of the Sunday Feasts. Now it is fire season, though, and they have had to move up to the ridge, where most of us live, and they are a few feet away in their tent. We can hear them talking and they can hear us talking, and when John wants to come over he sits in his tent and yells, "Knock knock, is it cool to drop by?" When he drops by it is always a pleasure. Today he read me his rewritten version of the Declaration of Independence in answer to my questions about what he thinks of revolution. In John's Declaration of Independence it says, "You senators and congressmen, are you sincere?" He wants to give every chance. John is about twenty, and he is presently a runaway from reform school somewhere, where he was first sent at fourteen for stealing a motorcycle and then, after his first escape, for stealing a car. He is expert in botany and zoology, completely knowledgeable about rocks, soil, and the ages of the planet. Unlike the rest of us, he does not feel easy about taking things for free. He will call out, "Knock knock, Elia can I borrow a joint?" and then, after taking some grass will say, "I consider this a debt. I consider I'm in your debt." On the other hand, there is a redheaded kid who lives nearby who has asked for dope two or three times a day, has used our kerosene and stove, but has managed to retain a surliness almost abstract in its forcefulness without meaning.

Scarcity, as a catalyst of human relations and a gentle reminder of the existence of the daily body and its daily needs, is most evident at Wheeler's. It is generally understood that everything is shared. For the most part no one is too worried about being robbed or too miserable when it happens. If you leave your campsite for two nights running, your tent and all belongings could be gone, although it is more likely you will find someone has moved in. Someone came up here a while ago with the idea of dealing some grass, because there is never enough grass here and it is a long ride to San Francisco. He made it known he was here on business, got a few people stoned so they could see how good his stuff was, and quoted them some price. When these people were satisfied as to its quality, they took all his dope and told him to leave. Barter is acceptable, but the money cycle is usually bypassed in the internal workings of the Ranch. Linda has told me that in the town where she was born, Osaka, Japan, she used to hear, all through the night, sharp hollow thwacks of bamboo poles being struck together. The sound seemed to travel through the streets until dawn. She found out the local cops used this method of warning thieves they were approaching, so the thieves could finish up and clear out. Also, all the homes wealthy enough to attract burglars would, as a matter of nightly ritual, put a little money in a particular spot near the window, just in case they were visited. If they were, the thief would take this money and move on. If the money wasn't there, he would go through the house looking for whatever he could find, taking it all. This all seems extremely sensible and a non-bureaucratic method of distributing the wealth. Here one gives anyone whatever is asked for with the knowledge that after a while equal distribution will have been attained and one can start roaming tent to tent in search of food and dope and they will be provided.

There are several hundred stray starving cats on the property and you pass them walking alone and scrawny at the sides of the paths. They will look up and hang a long still gaze at anyone passing until it is apparent that this person will not feed them. At night they nose through the trash and often slide into the tents to steal food. There is one particularly ugly cat with a nose strangely mapped in pink and black making it look as though part of its face has been eaten away. This cat has one pink eye and one blue eye. It is tiny and white, looks sick and carries burrs and insects in its coat. This cat is usually at our tent. Last night it was sleeping at my feet, warm in the blankets. I opened the flap of the tent and threw it out.

Green slugs, huge, lugubrious and pulseless, were softly inserting themselves into our living space. All over the property, hungry natural things are making their way to containers of food. Last night we heard a girl in perilous excitement screaming, "Get outta here! Get *away!*" She was addressing herself to two horses who were pressing in on her, after the grains she kept in her tent, which was actually a tarpaulin slung over a branch. After a while, snorting and bored, they left to rummage through the Pine Grove, where the largest settlement of shelters is. This morning the girl's tent was pulled down by two cows after the same grains. She chased them with a stick and one was rolling slowly ahead of her with pieces of her laundry pasted to its face.

Night: fog rolling in in dusk of more and more fullness to a resounding round black around a clouded pale moon. Here and there party sounds squealing and blossoming all over Wheeler's. Just before, we came upon three stoned kids who asked our names by flashlight, saluted good-bye with waves of flashlight. Many visitors to here see the residents as wide-eyed animal children, a tribe captured at birth by wolves. I feel this too a lot of the time. A sluggishness and unconcern for one another, fear of one another in crowds. Of course this is only some of the time with some of the people. There are many enclaves of friends throughout the night under trees, chatting, cooking.

June 31. Yesterday was very good. There was a feast, as there is every Sunday, and then a festival of music. The feast was sparse, only three or four things passed among us as we sat in the road, because last month's welfare money is almost gone and this month's is almost here. A pot of brown rice, a pan of fried potatoes and onions, and a stack of chapati (an unleavened bread) were distributed to about forty people, and someone had a huge beautiful pipe with the head of a Spaniard carved in the bowl, which he filled and refilled with grass. Some large dogs fought over potatoes and we watched them for fifteen or twenty minutes. There was not much talking throughout the feast, except when friends from the city came down the road and were greeted. There was beautiful carnival music played by Ramon on his accordion, and ten guitarists played along.

Bill Wheeler, who inherited this land, sat on a rock and told stories about his trial at the Santa Rose courthouse, where the People of California have brought suit against him for allowing over a hundred people to live on his land in structures that do not meet the requirements of the building code. He was very depressed about the trial, especially the fact that his daily attendance is required and for weeks he has had no time to work in his garden or do his painting. There is a large house on the hill which he built some years ago and which he is not allowed to sleep in, because of its legal and technical deficiencies. It has a sign on the door saying PLEASE DO NOT TOUCH THIS DOOR. BILL WHEELER MUST HAVE A PLACE TO DO HIS ART. Inside the walls are covered with large abstract paintings which you come upon when walking in that area and which appear through the large window-walls as strange artifacts of the life of the mind, seeming somehow historical and forgotten on the ridge overlooking two canyons. I have wondered about the man who was painting them and was locking this single door on these acres of land he himself has opened, Bill Wheeler, and meeting him yesterday was impressed by qualities that make him the perfect overseer for an area of anarchy. That is, Wheeler is attempting to do what his mind, higher emotions, and close friends tell him is the right thing to do, something which is being done at this time in only one or two other places, which is illegal and difficult— opening his land for habitation rent free to whomever wants to come there and allowing them to live exactly as they please, not communally or with purpose, but as the mood strikes them. At the same time he is attempting to retain the mannerisms (usually the first things one surrenders in any new living situation) that made him so happy with himself when he was rich and cynical in Connecticut. This, the keeping of the old ways, causes some people to pity him, mentioning the fact that Wheeler is not a "high" or "spiritual" cat in his rapping, and the stories of Wheeler riding a horse around the property, galloping up to clusters of people and telling them to put out their fires or save their water, and Wheeler's raucous consistent horniness, bad temper, loud voice, and snottiness, but it now seems that these are the things which Wheeler has found it necessary to take with him outside the law to keep him with himself and capable of struggling to keep the property open and anarchic. When we met him he was drinking beer and wine to calm himself because he had seen a cop with binoculars standing on Kelly's land, which borders Wheeler's, watching the feast for hours. The land has been raided twice, surprisingly by surprise (as there is a long gutted road leading into the Ranch, impassable at speeds over five miles an hour) but the only thing the police have been able to bust for was two juveniles.

The property is enormous and whoever is here to avoid the army or arrest in some other place usually makes it to the bottoms of the canyons where it would be impossible to find him. There is always grass here, however, and at the feast there was a lot of it, and I think if anyone gets busted for dope on the property, Wheeler is busted too, because the land is still in his name.

We visited Wheeler in the tiny round house where he is allowed to live, since it passes as a temporary structure according to the building code, and he was drinking this beer and wine, murmuring furiously about the pigs and Kelly, and reading an article about Wheeler's in *Harper's* magazine. He said he is a very happy man since he opened his land. Said, "Now this is the perfect mixture of the city and the country. You have people all around when you want people and you don't when you don't." I asked if he ever desired the place to be more together in the sense of having some purposeful group work being done. He said no. People will do what they want. Work is essentially for those who like work, is only one of the alternatives open to man for the killing of time in the world. He said, "Open land is when you never tell anyone to leave. The difference between never telling anyone to leave and telling one or two people to leave now and then is enormous. The difference between life and death. Never tell anyone to leave. Even these guys that rip people off. When we find out who it is, we don't tell them they have to go, but they usually do. Because the vibes get too heavy for them. The personal vibes from the neighbors." He said there was a seventeen-year-old meth freak up from the city to cool out, who transcended ripoffs altogether. He would go into tents and cabins and destroy everything in sight, start fires, smash possessions. If the occupants were in occupancy he would beat them up. He had the strength and determination of total insanity. After his tantrums everyone would try to talk him down, smooth him out. It seems after incredible amounts of this bullshit they still didn't evict him. But one day he ransacked the tent of an extremely handicapped arthritic girl, who was well loved by everyone who knew her. Kicked her out of bed and made her walk away, painfully, as fast as she could. Then Wheeler took him to a state mental hospital. While Wheeler was trying to have him committed, the kid was nodding. "Yes, yes, I'm crazy. He's right. Yes, I did that." But after Wheeler left, they interviewed the boy and found him not unwell, so several hours later he reappeared at the Ranch. Never kicked off, he finally got bored and decided to return to the city.

Wheeler has been in the courts off and on for three years now for permitting these hippies to come and build their beautiful, unsafe, unclean housing and live among one another. He says the court costs are very high and depress him terribly, as does the cost of the Empire Sanitary Service with its big red tank truck, which keeps four outhouses spic and span and supplied with toilet paper. "Empire Sanitary," says Wheeler, "is our ticket to ride." Men from the courts come onto the property all the time, taking pictures of piles of shit and putting samples in bottles, photographing pieces of newspaper and broken bottles, to prove the land is not fit to live on. There are also a lot of aerial photographs that these people take from helicopters and blow up to poster size for the People's Exhibits, showing half-constructed homes, homes of tin and cardboard, people giving the helicopter the finger, etc.

On the other side of Occidental, a tiny town of one short street completely populated by the owners of the town's three Italian restaurants and the families of the owners, is another place called Morningstar, at one time owned by someone named Lou Gottlieb, now deeded to God, also open land, also illegal. Gottlieb has been to court more even than Wheeler. Wheeler said he is worried about Gottlieb's health and peace of mind, because Gottlieb has become an open-land fanatic and defends himself in court and thinks about nothing else. He and Wheeler constitute a crusade for free rent. Wheeler looks and looks again out all the windows of his house, to see if the cop with the binoculars is still on Kelly's land. He is screaming, "Hide your piss and shit! He's got a camera!"

While we were there a kid in a Malcolm X t-shirt came to the door and cleared his throat. When someone comes to the door Wheeler usually moans over another stab in privacy's gash, but always lets him in. This kid had an infected finger. Wheeler examined it, said he didn't think it had staph, and gave the kid some soap to clean it and gauze to put over it. He said he has tried to get a doctor to come up here on a regular basis but has not been successful. When the kid left, Wheeler's baby, Raspberry, was pissing on Gay, Wheeler's wife. "Raspberry," he said, "don't you know they've got a camera?"

Carl: "I know this. I've worked all my life. I always made somebody richer and I always got cheated. I love nature, but I hate people. People destroy nature. But they can't destroy nature, and even if they do destroy it, it's always there and it will take care of them. I mean it will destroy them. Nature—the natural things— nature's waiting for the right time, then she'll come back and you won't know what happened.

[185   ]

"This land's been ravaged three times. I've watched it happen. That's what I love about you people, the hippies—you are to a great extent flower children. If you don't mind my saying so. You want to live in peace and quiet. You don't want to upset the place you're living in. As far as me is concerned. Oh yes. I know a lot of you people. You know that fella, Tex? I give him the hat he wears, that big hat." Carl is a very old man. His wife died in October. When he talks of her he cries. "What was good for her, that's what I wanted, and what was good for me, she wanted. Sometimes I thought she was the only decent person in the world. I brought her up here twenty-four years ago. From San Francisco. I guess, as far as me is concerned, it was an escapist idea. I wanted to get away from people. The rat race. It was a rat race even then. That was just before they dropped that bomb on the Japanese. God, I felt like a dog the day they had that on the radio. Can you imagine this country? I love you people. But I know they'll use force against you. That's always been the way with this country. They always use force. I was in the unions. I'm pretty well read up on labor history. Of course now the unions are mostly phony, but we had some very good. Do you know Harry Bridges? Walter Reuther? Eugene V. Debs? That man was in jail and he got a couple million votes for President *while* he was in jail. He was a great man. But they'll always use force. They'll always use that force." Carl drove us to the Ranch. He said to watch out for the people of Occidental. "I know how much they hate you. You know that." He told us about beatings he had gotten years ago, years ago, when he joined the salmon fishers' union in San Francisco, before he brought his wife to the country.

Of all the rare things that occur among mental men on the political earth, I have never seen anarchy before this place. By this I do not mean the conspiratorial politics of the anarchist left, which is in a sense a piece of the structure of the law, conspiring with the oppressors in a tight dance dancing its will into existence, but anarchy at peace with itself, separately and at peace occurring. And the result of this anarchy is impossible to imagine or to construct hypothetically. It is in fact the opposite of a reckless life, being almost completely cooled out and calm, a daily pressurelessness of living without statutes or any hierarchy of personal influence, one person over another. In this way Wheeler's, and the place on the other side of town, called Morningstar, are unique and opposite to other experiments of communal living. We are in a state of anarchy. Nobody can do anything that is wrong or illegal; nobody can do anything which will lead to his being kept out or thrown out. Think about how rare this is. It is the source of all ease and happiness in living with others.

And here we are, Linda and I, having the time of our lives on this overpopulated hillside. Here we are safe without hassle, useless, unproductive, not called on to do this or this on this area of land which has been cleared of government.

July 3. I have noticed two things, especially, while going about the intended project for which I bought a little tape recorder in the city, the interviews of my neighbors at Wheeler's. Usually, these interviews do not come off as I am so embarrassed about the implications of recorded conversation that I always turn the machine off and never ask questions. Generally, Linda and I will have the potential interviewee over to our tent for dinner, we will all turn on, sit and eat, mumble giggling for a while, then he will leave and we will roll into our privacy. But with the lack of actual individual interviews notwithstanding, I have learned these two things: 1. Nobody talks about or is very interested in his own past any more. That is, when people of my age settle down to earnest discussion, which is not that often, we don't talk about our childhood, the developments of various neuroses, our psychoanalytic history, or the story of personal crises. A few years ago this is what people talked about. Now you do not hear life stories at all, you hear the exposition of *beliefs*—religious, political, dietary—and what is foremost in people's minds is not themselves, as narcissistic gazers in deep evolving self, not one's private mind, but what they believe. 2. There is a class line that runs among the hippies, determined by wealth and breeding. At a place like Wheeler's, poorer, poorly educated freaks show up. They are actually broke (aside from the desire for voluntary poverty, shared by many, these poorer ones are in fact without resources); most are on welfare or do migrant work in orchards and canning plants. There are so many here who have been to reform schools and prisons. These are not the hippies who are in Europe and doing their bumming there. Those are the richer ones. These poor kids are also not the ones in college and involved in radical politics. Freaks with less money in their families are more amenable to religious fashions than to political fashions. They hold radical beliefs and feel more strongly and deeply than college students a desire for total equality among the people in the world; but unlike freaks of the middle class they never use phony violent revolutionary rhetoric. This might be because they have available to them personal recollections of violence and physical pain. They are also more honest dealing dope, more honest talking, less grotesquely dressed than richer freaks.

There is also an upper class among hip people. It is made up of those who inherited their wealth and those who acquired it in the entertainment, entrepreneurial, or drug fields. These people are sometimes called hip capitalists and are generally more conspicuous pigs than older monied Americans. They are self-indulgent, self-ish, will cheat you and often do, even on an ounce of grass, and they are responsible for such ugly places as Sausalito and all those cute towns along both the nation's oceans. The nicest thing about these people, as a class, and they are a class, is that when a group of radicals needs money for sustenance or political activities these rich hippies are available to be ripped off, as they will probably not call the cops. Too dangerous for them-selves.

Hip capitalists are also notable for the oppressive working conditions and low wages they offer in their perverted head shops and souvenir stores. Poor hippies are notable for the element of criminality they have brought to freak culture, which, while it was all middle-class and all supported by money from home, was not full of robberies and muggings, etc., but also was not full of generosity, which these ones have brought to it.

Certainly nothing just written has any meaning ex-cept that there is a salutary effect on people when, even for six months, they do not have things and money in their possession. I did not know this was true, but now I have learned that the very ones who are called free-loaders, ripoffs, lazy hippies and useless acid heads, the ones that all the advertisements for new communes in the underground papers ask *not* to come around, are the unbelievable sweetness of travel in America and the home of what spirituality there is in the country that has no laws.

The man from Empire Sanitary was here yesterday, sucking up the outhouse shit with his sluggish hose into his big red tank truck and leaving each Empire outhouse smelling sweetly, flyless and full of toilet paper and toilet seat covers, thereby extending our claim that we are in compliance with health and sanitation regulations. He is a welcome sight to those of us who use the outhouses, which are standing drunkenly on hills and mounds around the property, institutional-gray painted with the word EMPIRE stenciled on each one. Swarms of flies were in there before he came, and no one would use these places. Jose Soto, who plays the accordion, wishes we would not use them and attributes his great peace of mind and excellent health to the fact that he shits in the earth once a day, respectfully, with prayer, completing the beauty of the order of his creation by producing food for the ground. When he speaks of this, showing with his hands how he gently spreads the earth to receive his offering, I often feel he has actually discovered a lost element in the small world of true things, a central fact of life lost to civilized, toilet-trained man, and whenever some aspect of the multiform insanity of the law or the war or the cities is mentioned in conversation, Jose will shake his head sadly and say, "It's the toilet training. They can't help themselves. They do not feel beautiful; they feel they have to *do* something, because they just don't know that man is beautiful as he is, and all he has to do is to shit. Man is a shitter. That is his job. He does it for Mother, sweet Mother."

July 5. Bill Wheeler's young wrangler face with long Smith Brother beard wrinkled up amused and he said, "Wowee! It's just like the Wild West!"

A green pickup truck came speeding jolting halting and speeding past the goat pen where Linda was washing the dishes. I saw Bill run out in front of it, down near his place, and yell at the driver to get his car off the ranch. He dislikes to have motor vehicles past the front gate, because they create dust and he finds them ugly and distressing. The driver, a straight who seemed to be drunk, leaned out his window and told Bill to get fucked. Then he turned off the road and came barreling up the slope, mashing down shrubs at my tent, where I was calm and nodding, watching immense sunset set to the tune of my own humming. There were two men in the truck and from where I was they seemed to possess grim, composed expressions on their faces. I thought they were going to drive into the tent so I said, "Hey, you can't drive here." Then some redheaded guy came out of the trees, naked, with a little flute to the tune of which the sun was also setting, and he also told them they could not have their truck here. They yelled something at him, low and unyielding, and he said, "Be cool, Brother," which these characters were obviously not being. By this time, through the even sea of my evening high I was beginning to feel that these men were dangerous pigs who had come to hurt someone. I ran after the truck, almost caught up but they reached the top of the hill, where Bill's studio is, and shot down the other side. Bill caught up, was muttering, "Fucking cars, fucking cars," and he and I and the redheaded guy sort of walk-ran along, expecting they were on their way out and that was just as well. Then we heard shots and nude bodies were running toward us raising pats of dust, screaming, "Take cover! They're firing on us!" Bill asked if anyone had been hit. These people said they didn't think so. Bill, for some reason, said there was nothing to worry about and eight or nine of us walked up to where the cars are parked, where people were lying on their stomachs under the cars, behind trees, peering out of the outhouse door. But the shots had stopped and we could see the dust from the truck far away on Kelly's land. Someone said he had seen the truck trying to run a yellow Chevy with two hippies off the road. I wanted to go see if these two were hurt, but no one felt like driving up the road. Said it was bad karma to follow violence uphill. But one guy with a Volkswagen said he would drive. Bill and I went with him. In the back of the car I was looking around for a weapon, but the car was full of baby accessories— diapers, plastic tubs, Ivory Snow (which we discussed as one of the components of homemade napalm, as it forms a gelatin when hot that will stick to whatever it hits), little hats and shoes, a small shovel which was soft and red. The truck had been going at 50 to 60 mph, and that is an impossibility on the road going into Wheeler's. They had gone right through a barricade of bales of hay which Tex and some others had set up when the truck first entered the property, at top speed, and someone said he thought the one who wasn't driving, the one with the rifle, had hit his head on the windshield when they hit these bales. Later on, up the road, we saw they had lost their muffler. The two boys from the yellow Chevy came upon us, were bewildered and scared, on foot, off the road; said the truck had not fired on them but had wrecked their car.

At the main gate, on Coleman Valley Road, we got out of the car to inspect the damage. The truck had gone through this gate and it was exploded at the hinges. Bill said he put this gate up last year, was pissed off. This is when he brightened at the thought of the Wild West, hanging onto the gate slats and swinging like a maniacal chimpanzee, yelling, "Eee-ow! It's the O-o-ld West!" We did not see the truck or any traces of it, and this made us feel the need for further chase, although we didn't want to catch up with the truck. I thought we should call the police. Bill said, "I never call in the pigs. Never cooperate with the pigs. Not in my whole life." I said I never cooperate with the pigs, either, but that in this case, with these guys drunk and armed, hunting for hippies in the evening calm, and in this county, Sonoma, with its great number of hippies on the roads, alone, with their backpacks, hitching, it might be a good idea to have the pigs remove the danger from the area. We did not have to say who we were. After a short consideration of all this, we drove into Occidental and called the Gurneyville police, who guessed the shooting had been at Wheeler's, though Bill repeatedly refused to say who he was or where it had happened. Then we went to Morningstar, to see if the truck had been there making the rounds. It had. It was already gone when we got there. Some people sitting around a stove told us about the truck's visit and said the men had appeared to be unhappy about something.

I am very tired. These irrational violent pigs. Very afraid of these types.

In the car I noticed that Bill is fanatically ecological, and notices signs of destroyed ecologies all over the road, constantly interrupting what he is saying to say, "Fucked. It's all fucked over . . . look at this . . . look at this . . . fucked over, treeless. . . ." This is not hard on formerly peaceful Coleman Valley Road, where huge Cats with rollers and graders sit by the side of the daily expansion work which is being done so the loggers can cut the bigger trees, which they have a tough time coaxing around narrow curves.

July 6. Had a dream last night which I am ashamed to note, it being another time, in wake and sleep, when I have been made a fool of. I will say, though, that at the end I was in a giant double movie house, and "Dr. Jekyll and Mr. Hyde" was playing in filmy undulations on one huge screen while on the other, the one I chose to watch, a small black-and-white movie without people was shown. Both films had large audiences of men in conquistador costumes, wearing round metal helmets and sitting cross-legged on the floors. I thought these men were actors in a play that was being done in another part of this gargantuan entertainment palace that I was dreaming. I got into the theater free, I remember, and as always happens when I get in free, I wanted to leave because I hated the movie. It was a smoothly rolling montage, hour after hour, an epic, of boxes and crates in a warehouse. Whole families were there, and they seemed to love it.

Earlier in this dream, or possibly later, I was walking around North Beach in a pea jacket and two sweaters, wondering to myself if I was holding any dope. For some reason I could not be sure whether I had any. Kept running into the police on every corner. An old, fat man asked me to act as his bodyguard while he went to the bathroom. The bathroom was a hotel luxury bathroom. This man said he was a gangster and people were after him. In the bathroom, the attendant had a gun under a towel, attempted to kill my employer. I left immediately and do not know how it turned out.

When I woke up I told Linda about these dreams. We decided the two films in one theater, and "Dr. Jekyll and Mr. Hyde," were symbols of the fact that I am a Gemini. Often I have tried to use my dreams, to learn from my dreams, what to do, what I have done, what will come about, but I have never succeeded in answering any questions from my dreams. But waking up, and opening the flap of this tent, and the land sloping down into the canyon, and then another ridge, clearly delineated in the morning or under fog, and telling one another all these dreams, Linda's dreams, my own dreams— what a waking up!

We went to take a shower, Linda was shy about taking showers here at first, at the hose by the goat pen, where everyone goes to bathe and get water, wash clothes and dishes. She had many incomprehensible reasons for her shyness, which I did not understand, though I did understand the shyness. I told her she has the most beautiful body at Wheeler's Ranch. I said it was perfect, slim, graceful. Now she takes two showers a day. Can't get clean enough, and I can go down there to watch her rubbing soap over her smooth, spotless body in slow ellipses while ten or twenty people with buckets and babies shift from foot to foot around the hosing area.

July 7. Just returned from a pleasant walk in the murk down to the community kitchen and past it. Met a guy at the kitchen who said he is hiding out from the Berkeley police for some recent riot there. He said he is the one who stood, at some point in the speeches of a rally, and yelled, "Take to the streets!" and he is afraid they will want to prosecute him for inciting the crowd to riot. I asked him to tell me if it was a good riot. He said they broke a hundred and twenty windows on Telegraph Avenue, "before they even had a chance to call the pigs." This guy kept saying things like "too many people talkin' revolution, not enough willin' to go out an *start* one," implying that he was. Berkeley riotscape comes to mind, the 120 poor disposable windows of Telegraph Avenue metamorphosed from broken to unbroken to broken again. Berkeley, supposedly the freak center of the U.S.A., is actually a small town with twenty bookstores and no moods, only paranoid twitching expectation. In the thick fog with dream trees rolling through and coming upon a gray textured dream house grazing on a hillside of shrubs I took a long walk to give my high some exercise, as recently I have been stoned and lying down in the bad weather.

Linda met a chick today who was almost hit by the gunfire a few days ago. This chick's friend found the bullet, which was imbedded in a tree, and put a hole through it to make a necklace for her. Nevertheless, the chick sees the incident as a warning and is going to leave Wheeler's soon. Walking around, we have seen incredible structures rising all over the land. Houses built of old wood, pieces of tin, plastic, cardboard, canvas, with walls of old windows. New gardens are being started. Squash, tomatoes, carrots, corn. Bob is perfecting manure teas to make marijuana grow faster and stronger. They are building a church overlooking one of the canyons. Complete avoidance of crisis consciousness. General opinion is that Bill will lose in court, and the cops will come up and tear everything down, but building is going ahead in any case.

July 9. Freezing from washing the dishes in freezing evening fog. Relax in my little green tent, gauze door open onto rolling hillside misty under nature's fumes, filling my tent with cigar smoke. Isolated coughs and guitars and babies' requests, and on the land I have come to be known as The Typer. When anyone asks for me, people say, "You mean The Typer?" Bart, formerly Baker Bill, gave me a typewriter, a Rocket, that someone gave to him. But I tell everyone, because it's the truth that Linda is the Typer. They say, "Are you The Typer?" I answer, "No, that's my old lady."

We went on the shit run today. I was at the barn this morning throwing out the garbage, begging for a ride into Occidental. The community truck was scratching, as it does, in preparation for a start. Bill said it was going on the shit run. I was talking into going. Linda came too. The idea is that we get all the horse shit we can use, for the many organic gardens on the property, in return for cleaning out the stables of the Joy Ridge Ranch and replacing the manure with wood chips. It was a beautiful ride to this ranch, a cold day like autumn, and we passed a joint, murmuring things like, "Beautiful day for a shit run. Good shit-run weather." We got there, and we were not greeted or observed by anyone on the Joy Ridge Ranch, which was deserted and without life except for clumps of nervous, jaded horses all tied to fences or trees blinking and shitting. This outside shit is reserved for a second shit run each week and we were not concerned with it. Tom drove the truck into a light, wide, tan building with yellow straw on the floor and beautiful saddles, bits, whips, on nails in the walls. We cleaned the stables with pitchforks and shovels. There were twelve stalls, but two were occupied by horses and for some reason the horses had been locked in, so we didn't bother with these. There were seven of us, and two were women and one guy seemed to be very stoned and could not move well, so it was a fairly long time before we got the stables cleaned, threw the compost of shit and straw onto the truck, put two wheelbarrows of wood chips into each stall, and raked up the floor of the building. We were not tired when we were finished, though, because it was a cool day. On hot days, they say, the shit run is unbearable. We had a good time. On the way back to Wheeler's we saw a lot of hay by the side of the road. Earlier we had seen two men heaving this hay onto their truck, because it had fallen off at the curve. All this hay was left. We stopped the truck and threw bales and handfuls of it onto our truck, over the shit. One guy lost a bag of food which he foolishly left on top of the shit and it was covered with hay. Then we climbed back onto the sweet-smelling, milk-tasting hay and drove it bouncing over the terrible Wheeler's road, shit camouflaged with hay, into the Ranch where people greeted it, jumping onto the hay for a short ride, happy to see that the shit run was back.

I just remembered the only human life we saw at that stable while we were obtaining the shit. Two kids, about thirteen or fourteen years old with blond crewcuts and girlish, pleasant faces, came bicycling up to us and told Tom they knew a way he could make two, three, maybe four dollars a day cleaning stables someplace. He said he didn't need the work and they bicycled away, uncomprehending, superior, ringing their bells, into a carport.

July 11. Have not read a paper for over a week. No one here has any idea what is going on outside the Ranch. We are sensitive to the nuances of the news, though, and are confident that if anything important should happen in the world, the amazement of men in the world will reach us.

Met a fugitive from Miami dealing named Arthur yesterday. He was hacking at branches for a lean-to, stoned, looking as though he were about to do himself damage with his machete. Has a chick who reads cookbooks all day, smoking and snoozing, going all the time, saying, "Listen to this one, Art. Cocido. One can tomato paste, one pound fresh pork, one pound stewing beef, one pound ham. . . ." She is from New York. Art said he left Miami after a second ripoff of his house during which he was shot at, knocked unconscious with the butt of a shotgun, and robbed of a houseful of grass. Decided his karma was fucked up because he was becoming greedy, dealing too much and never knowing what to do with the money and it actually made him uncomfortable to have the money. He now plans to establish connections for buying and selling in San Francisco, and do a "rationalized dope thing," setting aside maybe six months for concentrated hustling with the goal of putting together enough cash to buy land which he will then open to anyone who wants to use it. Feels this is a religious obligation of some sort, having to do with his karma. We talked for a long time, all afternoon, and when we noticed the fog enveloping us, closing us off from more and more of what was around us, his lean-to was not done. I asked if I could help him, but he was very upset that he had forgotten how to do that shit, as he used to do a lot of camping out when he was a kid. I told him he was obviously too stoned to handle it, but he said I was too stoned to know. I see this morning that he did finish his construction— a canvas tepee in high wet grass, looking solid and warm.

Arthur's chick has left him, taking her cookbooks and little things in a satchel, leaving slowly, topless and pendulous, down the dusty road past the goat pen. She said he was a bastard for bringing her here, there was nothing for her to do here, the other men on the land were trying to molest her. Arthur says he never understood her. Says she never did anything in the city, either. When he met her she slept all day, only leaving her apartment to shoplift and meet men. "I enjoy the company of a woman," says Arthur, "but sometimes they're more of a drag than a pleasure." Arthur came here to get his head together, play his bongos in the trancelike sunset and plan his future. Now that his chick has left him he finds himself unable to concentrate on these things and he wanders around the property from one area of population to another, kitchen to goat pen to pine grove, up to the front gate where the cars are parked and the new people are coming through, offering grass to the chicks he comes across and playing the bongos for them.

July 12. Went to imperturbable town today, had the mandatory dull treat, ice cream, and learned from the milling congregation of panhandlers that the cops were at Morningstar Saturday. Lou Gottlieb has just lost his case. God cannot own land. Everyone must leave the land, or Gottlieb must pay a fine for each person found on his property. They say Gottlieb is appealing this, as he has been for several years now. In any case, the cops told everyone to leave, because they will be back for a bust soon. While there they discovered some patches of marijuana growing which they ripped out of the ground, photographed prolifically and carried away with them. No one arrested Saturday but presumably

Gottlieb will be charged. Some people from there already seen drifting over to Wheeler's. It is too heavy at Morningstar for juveniles, draft dodgers and other fugitives at the moment, though most people prefer Morningstar to Wheeler's, because it has orchards and streams that are easy to get to.

At Wheeler's there is confusion about the details and even the actuality of the raid at Morningstar. No one knows a thing. This is always the case here with events and occurrences. Some people say they have spoken to people at Morningstar who also don't know a thing. Yet I have talked to people who say they moved from there to here because of the raid. Similarly, no one is aware how Bill's trial, or Gottlieb's trial, is going, and nobody had heard of the thing in Occidental when some hippie showed his knife to some straights who were threatening him. On the other hand, the people of Occidental are thrilled by this story. Linda was at the checkout counter today in one of the stores listening to some old woman tell the old woman at the cash register that she is afraid these hippies are going to break into her house and the houses of other people. "They won't be happy until we're all dead," the woman told the other woman. "That's the end result of all this welfare."

In all probability Wheeler's gets the ax pretty soon from the county of Sonoma, reasons stated being inadequate housing and sanitation. These are the incorrect reasons, because a work camp for loggers in the same area with similar housing would be given a small fine periodically and allowed to continue operation, while Wheeler's is threatened with bulldozer destruction. Everyone will be evicted; beautiful houses, beautiful gardens will be torn down, ripped out, destruction that has been accomplished in other places by the State to discourage the massing of the freaks; and the newspapers will carry photos and stories of the incredible filth and putrescence of the place, unbelievable to the people who read about it, who will say, "Why are these people trying to kill themselves like that?" So Wheeler's will not "work," will not graduate to institutional stature in the manner of Harvard or ever reap the rewards of prosperity or be a good little place to retire.

This is a problem in people's minds. The idea of the communes "working," flourishing, succeeding is always brought up, but this is beside the point in the case of the communes now existing in America. The success or longevity of the enterprise itself is of no consequence—many places do not even think in these terms, and the ones that do are the ones that are arranged for maximal functioning and this means rules, the exclusion of free-loaders, good business sense, so that if one of these places succeeds it is like a little shop or farm succeeding, and of course this can happen and is of no interest. No, what is essential is to expose ourselves to a life of voluntary poverty, or life for minimal cost, and a life of sharing, noncompetitive, co-operative, neighborly—to try out a life like this—because this is what it is, alone, that makes the commune endeavor an important thing in America. There is no sense pointing out that as long as these communes are existing within the framework of America as it now is, and are taking welfare and sustenance in many cases from the state, they are not "succeeding." It is important, rather, to know that the people on the communes are certain the world is entering a new age, that they are the nuclei of prac-tioners of a new trend of life that will prevail, without their being forced to engage in physical battle with the pigs. It is their belief that they are changing the world by the example of their own daily lives. Without saying this, nothing has been said to explain *why* so many people are changing their lives so radically, so amazingly, attempting the difficult task of sharing whatever they have, at all times, with their neighbors.

Therefore, it is more correct to think of the communes as they now are as an intermediate stage in the development *away*—at this time away is the primary thing—from American life and ideals of malicious competitiveness and the step itself is incredible and more than outweighs whatever weaknesses any communal experiment may have, and even outweighs the rapid collapse of any or all communal experiments now with us.

Back East

I am in New York.

What makes you think I was in all these places I say I was in? I am not in any of them now. I am in an apartment, in New York, living among insects in a mist of insecticide. I can look out the window and see the old people in the park, sitting in rows on benches, all with their backs to squares of lawn and their faces turned to the traffic, all with the newspapers, reading the newspapers, learning, learning, leaving at dark, visibly suffering on airless days.

I watch a lot of television; Linda watches television. We are always on the phone. There is no air and the city is skyless. In the streets I see men and boys it is possible to mistake for myself and think, when I see one of them, "I have gotten thinner; I am shorter; I am in a hurry." I thought I would come here and read my book, and sort this out and sort that out, and slowly come to understand the lives of myself and other people, in all our chosen ways of living which are crude, not understood. But I am not coming to understand anything, because these are all prehistoric lives we are going through, not written or read about, not seen. Instead, I am reading the newspapers, all of them, seven a day, and the world is split and incomprehensible in my thoughts. I see I have been doing this strange exploitation journalism, a book of evasions, about no events and no important dates, filling notebooks with gestures and phrases from out of the way rooms and places that are not in anyone's memory but mine. I want to know what I have done. What are all the names I have written compared with the names in the center of your mind . . . lodged and roaming imperious over your thoughts . . . the names in the news?

I have written this book in order to give a reasonable and correct account of daily life in a country where the idea of daily life is not in the minds of the people. The people do not remember, from day to day, that they are doing this important thing of daily living. In the center of their thoughts and knowledge are names that are *not* their own names or the names of their friends and events that are not events in their own lives. Actually there, in the minds of the people, in their conversation, in their letters and worries, filling the attention like inane music, are the news of the world and fantasy (movies, sinister lotteries). And this news and this fantasy, coming to the people from a very few, faraway sources, are the same for all the people in the country, separating them from themselves and the moments of their own lives and making the people believe that the news of the world and creatures of fantasy do comprise what is known as daily life. What is the harm in this? It is that the people have lost the means of concentration and will to control their lives and the things they use and have. They must be taken care of . . . and then they are taken care of . . . and they are losing themselves, they are far from themselves. They are learning to disappear before the images of more essential men than they themselves are, as though the existence of such essential men were possible and as though each old man in the park does not live in the center of the universe. And now, in New York, the pressure of the daily papers and daily deaths are once again upon us, and things we understood in complete simplicity when we were alone in the anarchic communes and thinking slow enough have all been torn into, leaving

[205   ]

no exact thing I can say at the end of these stories that I am at this time sure of. Looking for an emblem of some kind to put at the finish of a book like this I am finding everything, every chance flash recollection from whatever place is perfect, nothing is not perfect; they are all just as good because there is no inevitable last thing in a list as this was, of this thing and this thing and this thing, each separate and following each, like a long file of eyewitness car-crash testimony or a list of the states and their capitals and products. But there is one story that is easy to see as the last in the list, for whatever it is worth, coming back to a place and feeling that all this traveling did not change or supersede, and that is the story of taking Iris in.

Taking Iris in . . . when I first met her years ago at the Pentagon, in the middle of floodlit night, distributing those loaves of bread and packs of cigarettes to the demonstrators between military attacks, laughing in a big fur coat, sympathizing comforting . . . always a little insane, with such a beautiful face like a round baby, always politician of insanity, always like speeding on ethereal pure speed, taking incredibly fast connections, connecting everything, making everything into a wide system of the spirit and the world's strange facts, only human ever to speak in normal conversation like a Rimbaud poem. . . . I had not seen her in a long time, but we had been writing strange letters. She got a job teaching French to kids in a private school, was demoted and demoted, finally lost the job because of coming insanity. Iris learned I was in Baltimore with Doug, decided to surprise, hitched down, surprise.

How hard it was to talk to her. She couldn't listen. I told her about what had been happening with me but she couldn't listen, kept looking around not focusing, nervous with all this news inside her to tell me, and everyone she met, which was as strange and unreal to me as my news was to her. She had the air of instantaneous shock and gripping eyes of someone who is there to save you, whispering secrets to me as though I were a prisoner and she was telling me how to escape within earshot of jailers . . . everything when she came to see me was so vital so essential to tell, but when she told it I didn't have any idea what she was talking about. Sky Daddy, Earth Daddy, centers and borders, trees in the middle of lakes, cosmic trippy conversation I couldn't relate to. Finally I decided she was tripping, asked her if she was, and she kept giving those evasive answers that the insane always do give, perfectly coherent to themselves but too fast, clear, and self-contained for me to understand. I was at first only helpless; then this helplessness became fear and anger, fear that she would take away my sanity and anger that I couldn't get to her, and actually there was envy, actually envy that she was going so fast and was so high.

I took her for a walk and she met my friends who all thought she was tripping too but when I told them she wasn't they couldn't believe it and had immense admiration for her, all of them wanting to hear her speak and ask her questions, but all of them finally losing interest and trying to escape saying, "Too heavy, too heavy." She had a little plastic container of jelly that was all gone but she kept sliding her pinky elliptically around the inside of the container and licking it, sliding, licking, offering the people she met a lick of pinky while she trapped them with her clear whap crazy eyes. Her clothes were fucked up, askew, ripped, mutilated, drawn on in crayon and ink, and she made an impressive sight: a beautiful girl with chopped wild yellow hair and clothes like a clown or war orphan, that incongruous. She had little dangerous habits, setting fire to the bed with incense sticks, bringing back from our walk a large thick branch and setting it up in a little glass of water from which it rose and engulfed the room in hanging branches and leaves impossibly tottering but secure in her glass, magic. She ate nothing, could not sleep, talked constantly, and looked as she had always looked, like a baby with baby mouth and nose and huge eyes.

The situation developed to where she was alternately laughing and crying, one leading to the other out of its own energies and not having to do with what was going on around her. We took her for a drive, she in the back seat, and she would be rapping, rapping, rapping, and then begin to weep and moan. I would say, "Don't cry Iris," and she would immediately stop, be still and calm, snivel, and then begin to laugh and laugh.

Interpreted everything, every picture, as a symbol and every noise as a message to herself and me, and she tried to draw me like a friend into this meaningful world, and then in the night when we were alone and I failed most miserably, completely freaking out with fear for my mind which she attacked with love and her pressing dreamlike sympathy, telling me to do this and that, things I didn't understand as things, to be freer, and I kept saying I am free, but she shook her head, explaining how I was not how she was approaching freedom, most desired freedom, which she yearned I could see to come to through her cosmology that she explained to me drawing pictures and writing poems full of puns which I envied but did not comprehend; and she answered no questions, even the simplest most slowly asked in a simple slow way, and I was lost. I finally could not bear to be alone with her; our eyes on two different realities, our bodies on the same floor, and I was confused, felt unequal to the task of understanding myself in the light of the new demands she was making on me and was still not certain she was crazy, not crazy at all, or only incredible. And I was pissed off so Doug and I took her to George's recording studio, barren cream colored with acoustical holes in the walls and ceiling, and George played her some music and that seemed to cool her out. Then I split and didn't hear about her for a couple of days during which time I talked about her to all the people who had met her and we came to the conclusion that maybe she was insane and I thought if that is insane it is partly good and partly bad. Then three days after splitting from her I got a call at Doug's place saying George says you know this chick Iris. The call was from some rock band which she had taken up with for these days and they said if you know her do you take responsibility? Background music for this is lousy flute and bongo music coming through the line like a dying party is going on. I said responsibility for what? And they told me Iris was in some trouble, was starting some fires out at their farm in the country and though they all dug her and loved her she was bringing the heat down on them. They had tried to put her on a train but the train wouldn't take her, also thinking she was tripping, saying we can't have a passenger on this train in her condition. Then they had tried to put her on a bus but also had trouble there, Iris singing and dancing, kissing strangers, and during an argument they had with the ticket man at Greyhound a cop had come over to see what was the matter and Iris had freaked out throwing paperbacks that she got off a spinning stand at him and then picking up the ready made sandwiches they have at the dining counter and throwing them at him. The boys told the cop this girl is not on drugs but was crazy and they promised to take her right to a mental institution, but now they didn't feel they could go through that with her and wanted to know if I had any suggestions. They said after all we are strangers to this chick. I said to bring her to where I was; they did and then immediately split, disappeared, mournfully looking back at Iris, who was even more disheveled, disarranged than before.

We talked about it and could not get a car to drive her to New York or anywhere else, and we were forced to take her to a hospital. We got in a cab. She was singing now and had a Realemon lemon juice plastic squeezer and squeezed it under her arms and between her legs saying, "A little sunshine here, a little sunshine here, umm," seeing everything talking about everything, so happy to see me and Doug but soon crying and laughing alternately again . . . saw the ugly lung-colored buildings of Baltimore all lined up the way they are, where most streets are a long wall and a long street like half a closed box, and said, "It is so bee-utiful, like new mown snow!" which we thought was incredible, incredible. Doug and I were watching her every action, fascinated and in love, as though we could watch her and learn how she does it, and the setting sun was hitting every top floor window, exploding in the grime as our cab went by, window to window with a toothache's rhythm, splash and rinse, and Iris seeing all these stricken buildings row on row would gasp like someone seeing an accident.

At the Hopkins hospital, where we were supposed to take her to the emergency ward psychiatric division, she got the idea and was scared. "I know what this is. I know what you're doing." But Doug said, "We are just here to visit a friend of mine in here, that's all," and she half trusted us though we did not fool her for a minute for she was, as they say, crazy not stupid. I said, "Doug will go see what room his friend is in while we go in here and look for a greeting card." So we went into the drug store in the hospital and I pretended to look at greeting cards but then she bolted for the door and I had to grab her by the arm and place myself in front of her, and she was crying and bawling, "I want to be free, don't you understand?" and of course I did understand; I didn't want to take her in there, I didn't want them to lock her up, but I didn't know what to do. I didn't know what to do. I said, "Don't worry, nothing will happen to you, Iris. I'm here to take care of you. I'm right here." She came into my arms. She squirted her lemon under my arm saying, "Umm a little sunshine here."

Doug came back pitifully sad made a motion for me to follow. We went down a corridor full of patients and moving beds and nurses and doctors flying along with their arms swishing, their coats flying, all flustered, and everything was green, sick, airless, and again Iris balked but Doug and I held her by the arms and she couldn't get away. We whispered in her ears, "Iris, we love you and we wouldn't let them do anything to you, you'll see," but we were lying because when you are taking someone there they are out of your hands, and methods you do not believe in are employed and nothing is done the way you know it should be, and you are giving up, giving over your friends to careless strangers.

Now a young chubby doctor appears at a door and beckons us into his tiny green and gray metal and rubber office where he sits behind a desk and smiles and I stand and Iris stands and Doug sits on a folding camp chair. "I know who you are," said Iris, immediately hating the doctor. "Yes," said the doctor, a little amused at her petulant anger. "You're the pigs," she said. "I wasn't born yesterday—the FBI, the CIA, right? The FBI, right?" He said, "This had nothing to do with the FBI, miss. This is a simple matter of mental health." Then they were in a fight and if they had been two politicians and she the politician for insanity and he for sanity we would have voted for Iris because she was so brilliant, funny, emotional, angry, right on top at all times of the slow befuddled chubby doctor. She was a beautiful woman with the stature of moral indignity, becoming alternately haughty and good-natured, angry and happy, willing to understand and yet holding back, not understanding and at some moments I must say I was afraid that she was not at all insane but was merely at a new level of genius and the doctor would have to say, "What did you bring this girl to me for?" Then she did the thing with the lemon, going umm-a-little-sunshine and squirting a shot right straight up her cunt and he said, "And what is that in your hand there, Iris?" so condescending. She snapped to instantaneous lucidity saying, "A plastic *lem*on, you asshole. What do you *think* it is?" He was convinced. Two gigantic nurses, thick even to the thickness of their fingers, came in, grabbed Iris roughly and dragged her off. Doug went with them because we wanted to make sure in this feeble way she would be treated well. I stayed with the doctor to answer questions about her family and the past of hers that I knew. I said, "I have known Iris three years and she is uncommonly amazing, so I didn't know if she was insane or had developed a new style of presenting herself." He smirked, said, "Looks like she has taken a lot of drugs. Yes," he said, "that definitely is the problem. Without LSD this girl would not have snapped." I said, "She didn't snap," growing more and more fearful of this man. I was afraid and ashamed to be here having brought Iris, a friend I loved, to this place though I had not known what else to do. I thought there is no getting around it: we are freaks; we are the freaks, we are deformed in the eyes of these people growing more and more deformed daily as we attempt to lead reasonable lives and think reasonable thoughts looking for impossible freedom. I felt I had failed by bringing Iris here to enemies. There must have been a place we could have taken her to cool her out, calm her down, give her food and let her sleep a few days; but there wasn't. We were in the middle of a city, all harsh and impossible for Iris to live in.

Then I went with the doctor down the hall past sick emergency patients in crowded corridors looking at me and the doctor, looking with needles in their arms and feeble drool on lips. The place was a road of highway gray, painful to see. Iris in a place like this and did I bring her here? So careful we have to be, when we are at war with these other people and they will put us uncomprehendingly in such corridors and locked rooms. And now at the end of the corridor there is Iris in a tiny room whose thick padded door is open and we can hear Iris talking and laughing in her room. The light on the ceiling, two bars of white fluorescence, one of them faulty and flickering unevenly, is tentatively on and off, a palsied shaky consciousness. Iris was sort of talking to it, "I'm going to live right here in the sun," she said, "and grow grow grow like a flower, a bee-utiful flower," and then the light strained a little on, a little off, on stronger, off, on, and Iris observed this as though she were reading lips and laughed, was amused by the light's reply. Her clothes were off and she wore a hospital gown that was too short and opened in the front instead of the back and hung laundered and stiff over her. One of the large nurses said, "Tell me why you hippies always have such dirty feet." I looked at Iris' beautiful feet.

What is happening? I sat down on the bed with Iris and asked her how she felt. She grabbed me around the neck and drew me close to her and whispered quickly in my ear all these instructions. "Remember, keep your head clear and just be cool everything will be OK; you're OK, just be cool," and she breathed deeply through nose and mouth in a show of health and enjoying fresh air. "Ahhh, ahhh," she inhaled deeply. Then the light blinked and balked again and Iris looked up at the ceiling with conspiratorial confidence. "Oh, I know," she said to the light, laughing. When she was like this Doug and I were beaming with pleasure because there was such a pure simple joy over her face, laughing so simply and democratically with people and things alike, like a little girl. Then the nurse comes in with two pills, tranquilizers to put Iris to sleep, says, "Take these," and hands Iris a cup of water. Iris immediately becomes scared saying, "No, I don't want these," and turns her head definitely, conclusively to the side, her lips closed. The nurse said, "Take these or we'll have to give you a shot." Iris said, "I don't want anything. I know what those are." She didn't want to go to sleep. She hadn't slept in over a week, but she didn't want to sleep in that room, expecting Doug and I would take her out of the hospital at any moment, not wanting to miss our leaving. The nurse told us to leave, they were going to have to give her a shot. I said we would get Iris to take the pills if the nurse left the room. Iris became furious, uncomprehending seeing the pills in my own hand, and knocked them on the floor. She said, "I want to leave. Immediately." Nurse accompanied by three other gigantic women and two small black male nurses returned then with a needle, a cartoon of a needle immense and thick, pushed past Doug and me and attacked Iris by surprise, nurses grabbing both her

[214   ]

arms and one of the male nurses barreling into her stomach with his small head while he half circled his arms around her waist. Iris screamed bubbly shrieks deep and fearful while they trapped her face down on the tiles and stuck the needle in the back of her leg. Then they all left leaving Iris on the floor crying dumbly and in shock. Doug and I were standing unobtrusively in the corner impotent and self-hating, feeling that if we had seen a thing like this on the street it would be obvious what to do, but what was there to do? We all sat together then on the bed and Iris, getting slower and weaker, made another, a last, effort to say *everything,* so we would understand the way all things are connected in meaning and see certain signs when they were presented to us, but again we did not understand. On the walls of the room were messages scratched by the former inmates of the place (Calling Charles Atlas Calling Charles Atlas Get Me Outta Here), and all the pictures and words and diagrams had an occult and definite look about them. We got the feeling there was an alternate world and set of signs shared by the people who pass through this room including Iris, a tribal knowledge passed down on the walls in lists of numbers, lines from songs, schemata of the planets, and Iris was also reading them, nodding, nodding, rejecting some, approving of others, growing tired and beginning to yawn. Yawning, smiling, she said, "I want to go now, all right?" as though it was the end of a perfect day at the beach and she felt like having dinner. We said, "Go to sleep and we'll be right outside this door." She said, "All I want is freedom." She said it so calmly, with such a reasonable face and voice, just looking at us and saying simply, "All I want is freedom," then looking around in the pitifully small room with its coughing sun dying overhead and it seemed she was explaining something that was the answer to every doubt we had had about her, as though she had thought it too simple to bother even saying it until now. We said of course that is what we all want. She looked and looked right into my eyes, saying nothing, but with such a look of urgency and love; but even though I knew of course what it was all about, I couldn't give her freedom. It was so strange not to be able to give Iris her freedom, and I was so ashamed to see her in a prison, another friend of mine in one of these prisons, I said, "Now it will be all right . . . you know that Iris . . . we love you . . . you go to sleep."

Armed Love

Elia Katz

Startling and touching by turns, *Armed Love* marks the debut of a major new writer with a style and way of life all his own. Twenty-two-year-old Elia Katz started out from New York's Upper West Side in search of a communal life style with integrity and purpose. *Armed Love* is an expressive rendering of the quality of communal life from one end of America to the other: Baltimore, where Elia visits the largest acid dealer on the East Coast and his covey of women; Heathcote, a community based on monogamy but where everyone is deviously adulterous; Taos, where there is an ironic sadness in store for Elia; and finally Wheeler's Ranch in California, the ultimate confrontation between freedom